BULLDOG

SMART OWNER'S GUIDE™

FROM THE EDITORS OF DOGFANCY MAGAZINE

CONTENTS

Bulldog, a Smart Owner's Guide™
part of the Kennel Club Books® Interactive Series™
ISBN: 978-1-593787-58-5. ©2009
Kennel Club Books Inc., 40 Broad St., Freehold, NJ 07728. Printed in China.
All rights reserved. No part of this book may be reproduced in any form,
by Photostat, scanner, microfilm, xerography, or any other means,
or incorporated into any information retrieval system, electronic or
mechanical, without the written permission of the copyright owner.

*photographers include Tara Darling, Isabelle Français,
Carol Ann Johnson, and Alice van Kempen*

10 9 8 7 6 5 4 3

K9 EXPERT

He is compati-bull, socia-bull and lova-bull. Not surprisingly, he also broke into the top ten popularity list among breeds registered with the American Kennel Club. He ranked eighth in 2008, as compared to tenth in 2007 and sixteenth in 2003. It couldn't have happened to a finer, more mellow fellow.

Sports teams around the world have chosen the Bulldog as their mascot, to symbolize their players' stoic courage and strength. Quintessential politician Winston Churchill saw himself as possessing the tenacity of the Bulldog, and on this side of the Atlantic our own politicians relate to the Bulldog as much as they do to the donkey and elephant. If ever there existed an emblem to represent gritty determination, it would be the sourmug.

When it comes to universal recognition, the Bulldog is an icon, arguably the best-known breed in all of dogdom. As kids, we watched Saturday morning cartoons, enjoying a

bevy of Bulldogs brought to us by Disney and Warner Brothers, all determined to outfox the resident cat, duck, canary, or skunk. Sure, each one wore the obligatory spiked collar but we never for a minute thought any of them were nasty. More often, we rooted for them as the underdogs, teased mercilessly by diabolical rodents, felines, and waterfowl.

The Bulldog of today is a far cry from the fearsome beast of centuries past who was bred for the loathsome activity known as bull baiting. Once this grotesque spectacle was outlawed, breeders began addressing temperament issues, committed to producing a kinder, gentler representative of the breed. They were as determined as the dogs who were their passion, and their persistence paid off. The modern-day Bulldog is a sweet, loving and biddable canine, devoted to hearth and home, and a great children's companion.

Because his exercise needs are modest, he makes a perfect city dog, content in an apartment or house.

A few short walks a day are sufficient but if you live in a hot or humid environment, please be sure those walks are taken in the cool morning and evening. With the Bulldog's short muzzle and flat face, he doesn't tolerate the heat well.

Grooming is easily accomplished; a bristle brush and hound mitt used weekly will get rid of dead hair and make his coat gleam. Check his nails, ears, and teeth weekly; powder the folds of his skin and examine his feet periodically for sores.

Because of Bulldogs' big heads and body shape, they are typically born by C-section, an expensive procedure for breeders, which is reflected in a high price tag for puppies. Do your homework and find an established breeder for whom raising Bulldogs is a labor of love. Start with the Bulldog Club of America website where you will be directed to regional breed clubs, knowledgeable breeders who sign a code of ethics and rescue groups where older, deserving dogs in need of permanent homes can be found.

Responsible breeders will offer you references, a health guarantee, and a lifetime of after-sale support and mentoring. This new member of your family deserves nothing less.

Smart owners remain stalwarts

JOIN OUR ONLINE **Bulldog Club**

With this Smart Owner's Guide™, you are well on your way to getting your Bulldog diploma. But your Bulldog education doesn't end here. You're invited to join Club Bulldog™ (**DogChannel.com/Club-Bulldog**), a FREE online site with lots of fun and instructive online features like:

◆ **forums, blogs,** and **profiles** where you can connect with other Bulldog owners
◆ **downloadable charts** and **checklists** to help you be a smart and loving Bulldog owner
◆ access to **e-cards, wallpapers,** and **screensavers**
◆ interactive **games**
◆ Bully-specific **quizzes**

The **Smart Owner's Guide**™ series and Club Bulldog™ are backed by the experts at DOG FANCY magazine and DogChannel.com—who have been providing trusted and up-to-date information about dogs and dog people for forty years. Log on and join the club today!

of the breed forever. They don't see a snoring, gassy dog but a distinctive, aristocratic companion whose jaunty roll and wrinkled face grow more endearing by the day. To look at a Bulldog is to smile; to love one is a privilege.

Allan Reznik
Editor-at-Large, DOG FANCY

CHAPTER 1

FROM FIGHTER

Though the Bulldog may look tough and sport the shoulders and swagger of a muscle-bound weightlifter, this burly breed's temperament has evolved to be sweet and affectionate. Once bred to aggravate bulls to the point of collapse, the Bulldog had to be aggressive and tenacious, but breeders have worked to retain the Bulldog's characteristic look and spirit while mellowing the breed's temperament to create a suitable household companion. Bulldog lovers attest: The Bulldog makes a great pal.

That's not to say life with a Bulldog is a walk in the dog park, and smart potential Bulldog owners, or those just getting to know their Bulldog puppy, should be prepared for the Bulldog's unique and sometimes challenging temperament.

Bulldogs thrive on human companionship and truly enjoy being around all kinds of people. Their loyalty and strong affinity for people make them poor kennel dogs. Bulldogs prefer to stay indoors and spend quality time with their owners, rather than being left isolated in an outdoor kennel.

Bulldogs are very tolerant and patient with children, and love the company of other dogs and animals. They adjust rather easily to other house pets such as cats and birds.

it's a Fact

The Bulldog has served two terms in the White House! Pres. Calvin Coolidge had a Bulldog named Boston Beans, while Pres. Warren G. Harding had a Bulldog named Oh Boy.

They rarely fight among themselves, but when they do, it can be quite a battle! They are a very strong-willed breed and won't back down easily. They are extremely intelligent, quiet, and affectionate. You won't hear a Bulldog bark very often, but you will quickly grow accustomed to his loud snoring and belching! Surprisingly, many Bulldog owners find the breed's snoring rather pleasing, and rarely notice it once they have the dog around the house for some time.

Bulldogs easily adjust to an apartment setting or to country living with plenty of acreage to roam. They don't require an abundant amount of exercise and are quite content with short daily walks. They are not a very active breed, and individuals that are looking for a dog that is, should probably look elsewhere. Bulldogs are far happier relaxing in the comfort of your home; extended hours of ball playing are not for them. The Bulldog does enjoy short periods of play, and will be very content with as much human interaction and attention that a smart owner can possibly provide.

Because of their physical conformation, the Bulldog will frequently have difficulty breathing. This is particularly true during hot and humid days. Participating in any strenuous exercise should be avoided during these days. No breed of dog should be exposed to excessive heat, but Bulldogs suffer more than most during these uncomfortable hot spells.

Bulldogs are very heat-sensitive and require cool conditions, especially during summer. Bulldog owners often go to extreme

Meet other Bulldog owners just like you. On our Bulldog forums, you can chat about your Bulldog and ask other owners for advice on training, health issues, and anything else about your favorite dog breed. Log onto **DogChannel.com/Club-Bulldog** for details!

JOIN OUR ONLINE
Bulldog Club

lengths to keep their Bulldogs cool. Owners must also be careful not to overexert their pets on short walks.

An air-conditioned home is a far better place for your Bulldog to spend his day than being locked outside in the hot sun without adequate shade. Oddly enough, Bulldogs do enjoy basking in the sun as long as the outside temperature remains cool and comfortable. Dogs that are kept outdoors for long periods of time are also susceptible to more skin and respiratory problems.

MALE VS. FEMALE

A common question that is frequently asked by any new dog owner is which sex is the preferred choice. In most breeds, it doesn't make a whole lot of difference. With Bulldogs, males can be slightly more affectionate. All things being equal, it really depends on what you like and what you plan to do with your dog.

Are you purchasing the dog as a family pet and companion? Do you think you may be interested in becoming involved in dog shows or obedience? If so, you should let the breeder know what your intentions are or might be later down the road. This will help the breeder choose a dog that's appropriate for your lifestyle and one that will meet your expectations.

LOVE THAT MUG

As far as physical characteristics, Bulldogs come in a variety of dazzling colors. The most popular colors are white, red and white, brindle and white, white piebald, fawn or fallow. Color has little

Did You Know?

The Bulldog easily adjusts to an apartment setting or to country living with plenty of acreage to roam. They don't require a lot of exercise and are quite content with short daily walks. The Bulldog does enjoy short periods of play, and will be very content with as much human interaction and attention an owner can possibly provide.

importance when it comes to the quality of the dog unless you're planning on showing.

It's simply a personal choice and preference, although it is important to find a dog that conforms to the breed standard. You should rely heavily on the breeder's advice because they will obviously have more experience with the breed than you do. They will know how their specific Bulldog lines grow and develop.

Bulldogs enjoy chewing, so be extra careful with what you leave around the house.

High on the list of a Bulldog's favorite things are food and hanging out on the couch. Despite his imposing and stern appearance, the Bulldog can be a marshmallow of a dog. He loves to be with people, and his face can wear many expressions, from goofy to happy to incredibly sad. Along with the Bulldog's unique attributes, though, come unique challenges in grooming, feeding, conditioning, and training.

STUBBORN BULLIES

Bulldogs retain the stubborn and tenacious nature of their bull-baiting ancestors, if not their aggression. Known for their selective hearing, Bulldogs are a challenge to obedience train. They would rather make their own decisions about what to do, although they will do just about anything for a food treat. Otherwise, it can be difficult to motivate them.

Domineering as they sometimes may be, Bulldogs also can be clingy and overly dependent on their people. Bulldogs that are too attached to their owners often suffer from separation anxiety when left alone,

They might not be the most athletic breed, but they still like to run, *er*, walk briskly on occasion!

even for short periods of time. Once secure in their homes with their attentive families, a playful Bulldog, though, is enough to brighten any bad day.

Because his face is flat and wrinkled, the Bulldog is capable of many expressions. He can perk up his ears, tilt his head, smile, and look sad. Bulldog owners love how expressive their dogs can be.

COUCH POTATOES

Bulldog play can be vigorous, but Bulldogs tire easily, are extremely sensitive to heat and humidity, and in general, prefer a life of luxury to a life of exertion. Bulldogs bark if they think they have a reason to bark, but they probably won't keep it up for very long. It's way too much work. The same goes for chasing cats.

it's a
Fact

Every Bulldog is an individual and temperaments vary within even the same litter of dogs; however, the best indicator of a puppy's temperament is his parents, so take a close look at these dogs. Spend time observing and playing with the parents, if possible, and be sure to ask the breeder questions about their dogs' behavior and attitudes toward children.

Brace yourself for the high energy of a bully puppy.

BULLDOG QUIRKS

Every Bulldog is an individual and although temperaments tend to be predictable, many Bulldogs have quirks their owners are unprepared for. These characteristically low-energy dogs sometimes produce high-energy offspring.

The stereotype is a Bulldog couch potato, but a few are downright bouncy and have higher energy levels. Some also are afflicted with inexplicable fears and anxiety. Bulldogs are known to be courageous, but some of them are afraid of simple things, such as ceilings fans and plastic bags. These dogs often startle easily, and begin to show this trait at about six months of age.

Prospective owner should be aware that Bulldogs are chronic chewers, and this behavior is not something that's restricted to younger dogs. It will be important to provide plenty of rawhide bones and other chew toys to keep your Bulldog occupied when you're not home.

And then there's the snoring, the snorting, the snuffling, the sneezing, and yes—the gas. The sounds Bulldogs make when excited are often mistaken for growling, but they just do that because of their squished-up breathing passages due to their flat faces. It's like a bad sinus problem all the time.

Sure, Bulldogs have some issues. Not everyone is willing to put up with the pushy nature, the "won't-do" attitude, and the grunts, gurgles, and gas, yet Bulldogs remain among the most popular breeds of dog because so many find that wrinkly mug and happy-go-lucky personality irre-

sistible. The wonderful characteristics of a Bulldog—the mellow, friendly nature; the clown-like, affectionate, and laidback attitude—don't come preprogrammed into Bulldog puppies. What the dog turns out to be as a mature adult is largely a product of what a smart owner puts into him. All Bulldog puppies need early training and puppy socialization classes. That said, a well-socialized, well-trained Bulldog is an ideal family pet.

FRIEND OR FOE?

Maybe it's the look, maybe it's the brawn, but people often fear Bulldogs, which is something Bulldog fanciers find amusing. "It's an inside joke with Bulldog owners that we've got this scary-looking dog that really isn't scary at all," says Bulldog Club of America rescue coordinator Stefanie Light of Baltimore, Md. Yet, when it comes to other dogs, Bulldogs may not always be so friendly.

NOTABLE & QUOTABLE

Today's Bulldogs love people. They are very friendly, sometimes overfriendly in a slobbery way. They sit on your lap, and they wash your face for you. They get such human expressions; you can tell what they are thinking.

—*Bulldog Club of America historian Darlene Stuedemann of Clinton, Iowa*

"Bulldogs aren't supposed to be dog-aggressive, but some are," Light warns. "They usually won't start a fight, but they sure won't run away from one either. For some reason, some Bulldogs have trouble tolerating other dogs."

Mary Aiken a Bulldog breeder from Woodside, Calif., explains that intact males are more likely to be dog-aggressive than neutered males but training, socializing, and spaying or neutering your pet can go a long way toward modifying any dog-aggressive tendencies.

Don't necessarily expect super dog-friendliness either, however. "Bulldogs aren't the kind of dogs to run up to other dogs and play, and they aren't 'run with the retrievers' dog-

He might not strike you as the touchy-feely type, but Bulldogs are no less loyal and lovable than any other breed, indeed!

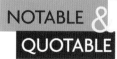

NOTABLE & QUOTABLE

Bulldogs like to be touching you, either lying next to you, across your lap, or at your feet.—Linda Shelburg, secretary and treasurer of the Bulldog Club of Central Iowa

The Yale University mascot is a Bulldog named Handsome Dan. The original Dan was an award-winning show dog in the late 1800s, owned by A.B. Graves.

park dogs, either," Aiken says. "They really aren't pack animals. However, they shouldn't be lunging at other dogs."

When it comes to their beloved bowls of kibble, however, Bulldogs may be less than benevolent about interlopers. "I feed all my dogs separately," Aiken says, a practice she recommends for all pet owners. "They don't have to worry about another dog intruding or about having to eat too fast. It lets them relax and it avoids problems because some Bulldogs can be sensitive about their food."

SNORING CHAMPIONS

Aiken can't stand the sound of her husband snoring. It keeps her awake all night. But the sound of seven snoring Bulldogs? No problem. "To me, it's normal background noise," Aiken says.

Bulldogs are notorious for the snuffling, snorting, grunting, and groaning noises that come from the shortened nasal passages and elongated soft palates characteristic of the brachycephalic (short-faced) breeds. All breeds with flat muzzles tend to snort and snuffle, and none more than the Bulldog. Light remembers spending the

night in a motor home with some friends and her first Bulldog, Chester. "My friends said they didn't get any sleep because it was like sleeping in a respiratory ward. It's really loud," Light says.

For those who find the snoring of their snuffly pets an insomnia-inducer, the answer is simple. "If it's too loud, don't let them sleep in the bedroom," Aiken says.

Yet people who love Bulldogs tend to become used to the sound and may eventually find it comforting. "It's amazing what people can grow accustomed to,"

Bulldogs are known for their loud snoring, but some owners find it soothing.

If you look beyond that infamous snarl, you'll find a heart of gold.

Light says. "I once read an old book about Bulldogs that said, 'Owners love his gentle snore,' which I have to say is, in a way, exactly right."

DON'T OWN A BULLDOG IF...

As great as Bulldogs can be, they're not suited for everyone. Think twice about getting a Bully if:

◆ **You want a dog that can go running with you.** As Georgetown University's website notes with respect to its Bulldog mascot, this breed can't even walk all that far.

◆ **You don't have air conditioning.** Unless you live someplace where daytime temperatures never exceed 70 degrees or so, a Bulldog will find your home too hot to live in unless you have central air conditioning.

◆ **You want a dog who's conventionally beautiful.** If you want a glamour-puss for a canine companion, a Bulldog is not for you. A true Bulldog lover sees this breed's inner beauty!

◆ **You want a great watchdog.** The Bulldog may look fearsome, but his temperament doesn't match his looks. This dog loves everybody, including intruders.

◆ **You don't want a Velcro dog.** Most Bulldogs want to be with their people 24/7 if at all possible. Being able to take a nap across your feet, on your lap, or in bed with you is heaven for these dogs.

◆ **You're a control freak.** Bulldogs love their people and usually are eager to please them. But many also have at least a bit of a stubborn streak in them and cannot be forced to do anything they don't want to do. So if you aren't one who can't sometimes go with the flow, you better find another breed.

True Tails

The Bulldog has a sense of humor and a mind of his own. He is a fun-loving companion that likes it when the people around him are happy, but the Bulldog can dig in his heels when asked to do something that doesn't fit his plans.

This gives the breed a reputation as bullheaded, but that's not necessarily fair. Gayle Justice, Bulldog breeder and owner of Puddin Hill Obedience Training & Pet Sitters in Waxahachie, Texas, sees through the bullheaded Bulldog stereotype.

"As for bullheaded, some are more so than others and some not at all," she says. "They each have different personalities, but they're fun-loving little clowns that love people. They'll do anything for attention, and that's what makes them so trainable," she says.

Amy Flanigan, owner of Civil Obedience Dog Training in Columbus, Ohio, has encountered the stubborn Bulldog attitude, but finds them easy to motivate with rewards. "Bulldogs don't like being forced to do anything," she says, "and they usually can't be made to in a physical sense; they're just too strong. Their necks are massive, making leash corrections ineffective, and they were bred to have a high tolerance for pain."

Bulldogs learn from experience that resisting their owners sometimes gets them what they want. Flanigan says, "I think this is why some people have labeled them bullheaded, when in reality the dogs just figured out what works."

Sue Alexander, owner of Dogs in the Park, a training facility in Guelph, Ontario, Canada, reframes bullheadedness as persistence, noting it's not necessarily negative. "A stubborn dog is also a dog that will keep trying, and trying, and trying," she says. And that's certainly true of Bulldogs.

BULLDOG DOSSIER

May we introduce this happy, gentle—albeit wrinkly—companion.

COUNTRY OF ORIGIN: England

ALIASES: English Bulldog

SIZE: males—50 pounds; females—40 pounds

COAT & COLOR: short and smooth; colors include white, fawn, brindle, piebald (white with patches of color), etc.

PERSONALITY TRAITS: kind, courageous, dignified, docile. Bulldogs are mellow and loving, jovial and comical, but can be stubborn at times.

WITH KIDS: excellent. Bulldogs love children and make loving, gentle playmates.

WITH OTHER PETS: generally good with other dogs, but may get aggressive and protect themselves if another dog provokes a fight.

ENERGY LEVEL: low

EXERCISE NEEDS: Though some would prefer not to exercise at all, all Bulldogs need at least a daily walk to maintain good health and prevent obesity, to which the breed is prone. Bulldogs should not be overexerted in hot weather.

GROOMING NEEDS: regular brushing to tame shedding. The Bulldog's facial wrinkles should be wiped daily with a damp cloth to remove dirt and prevent infection.

TRAINING NEEDS: Bulldogs can be stubborn training students and slow to learn, so patience and persistence are required on the part of a smart owner. All Bulldogs should be taught the five basics cues: sit, lie down, stay, come, and heel.

LIVING ENVIRONMENT: can live in any sized area, from apartments to a big house. Location is a factor, though, as Bulldogs do not do well in extreme weather, especially heat.

LIFESPAN: 8 to 10 years

BRIEF

During any extended period of time, it is quite common to see a breed of dog evolve into a totally different specimen than what it may have been hundreds or even thousands of years ago. In fact, it would be very unusual for a breed to remain consistent in type and temperament throughout its development. This is certainly true when studying the history and growth of the Bulldog.

The Bulldog, better known as the English Bulldog, has changed tremendously since its inception. Although there are some old attributes that can still be found in the breed today, Bulldogs that existed in the 13th century looked and behaved nothing like the type of dog we see represented in today's homes and show rings. Historians are fairly confident that the breed derived from ancient war dogs, or other types of old mastiff-like breeds. These war dogs were used by the British in times of battle and were excellent protectors of their master's property and flock. Still others believe that the true origin of the Bulldog is not entirely clear and are quick to point out the many loopholes that exist in some of the more favorably recognized theories.

Did You Know? **By the end of the 19th century, the Bulldog more closely resembled what it looks like today:** a dog of medium size with a heavy, thick-set, low-swung body; a massive, short-faced head; and wide shoulders with sturdy limbs.

BULL + DOG = BULLDOG

One safe theory is that the Bulldog was first developed in the British Isles and was originally bred for the sole purpose of bull-baiting, an extremely barbaric pastime that became very popular in England. Its popularity was so great that it became the national sport of England from around the 13th to the 18th century.

The first mention of the breed was in 1500, by one Cocke Sorrelles, who wrote of a man "with two Bolddogges at his tayle..." In the same year, W. Wulcher referred to the molossus, a mastiff-type dog that some experts say is the progenitor of the Bulldog type. The molossus probably originated in Central Asia and from there spread throughout the known world, contributing to the formation of many breeds along the way. One of these was the Bulldog, which reached its modern development over many centuries in England.

The early Bulldog was very different from the low-slung, shambling but dignified dog we know today. Those first Bulldogs were tall, with a smaller head than the modern version of the breed. They were certainly more fierce, given their use in bull-baiting.

Bull-baiting was an event that was usually held in conjunction with a series of boxing matches and took place behind rope enclosures in an indoor arena. To keep the fight on more equal terms, the bull was helplessly tied to a rope that was attached to a large hook in the ground. The sport involved the use of one dog, or a group of dogs, that set loose to pin and hold a bull by the ears and nose in front of thousands of screaming spectators. The nose was considered to be the bull's most delicate body part and where it was most vulnerable to injury. The dogs were specifically trained to attack this area. Despite its popularity, the event was a horrifying spectacle to watch. It was not uncommon for a group of dogs to be viciously killed or severely injured during a fight. Spectators often wagered on this tasteless event.

Did You Know?

In 1890, Bulldogs could have any of three ear types: rose, in which the ear curls softly around like a rose bud; button, in which the ear folds over, completely covering the inside of the ear; and tulip, in which the ear stands erect, with just the very edges and tip curving in slightly. Today, the rose ear is highly desirable, but some dogs still have button or tulip ears.

This breed's ancestry stretches all the way to 14th-century England.

Many bulldogs were killed during violent sports, such as bull-baiting.

A successful bull-baiting Bulldog had a thick, strong, overshot jaw to aid in grasping the bull; a short, flat muzzle to help air pass through the nostrils while the dog was clamped onto the bull; and a hard, rangy body, able to take a beating and survive being tossed into the air by an angry bull. Just as important as strength were courage and tenacity.

Beauty and conformation were of little importance to the Bulldog breeders of this early era. The breed's temperament of yesteryear was a far cry from the loving, loyal companion that's now cherished by fanciers world-wide.

BULL-BATING BAN

It wasn't until 1778 that an outcry against the barbaric nature of bull-baiting was finally acknowledged and acted upon by the Duke of Devonshire in Staffordshire, who officially abolished the harrowing sport. Unfortunately, this was not the end of the Bulldog's use as a fighting machine. Although bulls were no longer used, the fighting continued with rats, lions, monkeys, bears, other Bulldogs, and any other animal the English people could get their hands on. It wasn't long before dog-fighting and bear-baiting had taken the place of bull-baiting. In fact, these "sports" became just as popular—if not more so. Bear-baiting quickly developed into one of the most widespread baiting sports. Eventually, because of the high cost associated with importing bears, the sport gradually died during the 18th century.

it's a Fact

The Bulldog breed standard calls for a dog with a disposition that is equable and kind, resolute and courageous (not vicious or aggressive), and a demeanor that is pacific and dignified.

After bull-baiting and bear-baiting came to an end, many believed that the Bulldog breed as a whole would disappear. Fortunately, there were many individuals who were still interested in keeping the breed alive and were concerned with transforming it into a worthy purebred dog. These dedicated breeders set their sights on developing a breed that would be suitable for the family environment, as opposed to one that was a combative fighting dog. It wasn't too long before breeders switched from breeding for fighting and combat to breeding for showing and exhibiting.

By the late 18th and early 19th centuries, early Bulldogs were of poor quality compared to today's standards. Many of the fighting-dog qualities were still evident in the Bulldog's physical appearance. Dogs had small skulls, long noses, and no wrinkle covering the head. They were extremely crippled, and for the most part considered very unhealthy.

FIGHTER TO FAMILY COMPANION

It wasn't until the official Bulldog Club was formed in England that these poor physical qualities began to be worked out by concerned breeders and fanciers. Long before the English Kennel Club was founded, the Bulldog Club was the first group to attempt to standardize the breed, and the first to hold a conformation show for them in 1859. Jacob Lamphier is credited with drawing up the first official Bulldog standard in 1864, but it wasn't

SMART TIP!

If you are looking to add a Bulldog to your family, stop by a local dog show. Talk to the owners and handlers of competing Bulldogs. They are sure to give you some great advice. Just be sure to wait until after they have shown their dogs, when they will be more willing to talk and be less anxious!

until 1879 that it made it to print. The first real standard was the Philo Kuon, which was adopted in 1865 in London. Many of the first dogs who appeared in the show ring had splayed feet and bowed legs. To make matters worse, show judging was equally poor and did not in any way help with the breed's physical development. Even today, the Bulldog is considered a very difficult dog to judge correctly in the show ring, and years of dedicated experience are required to do it properly.

It is nearly impossible to mention the long list of influential breeders and dogs from England and America who are responsible for the Bulldog's development in the last 200 years. Some of the famous dogs during the late 1800s and early 1900s still have a stronghold on today's offspring, and many of the present top sires and pedigrees can still be traced to them. Some of these influential dogs include: Monarch, Donald, King Dick, Old King Cole, Crib, Rosa, Thunder, Sir Anthony, Brutus, and Sancho Panza.

In the 1800s, Crib and Rosa were two dogs that were considered the foundation for

JOIN OUR ONLINE **Bulldog Club**

Just how quickly will your Bulldog puppy grow? Go to Club Bulldog and download a growth chart. You also can see your pup's age in human years; the old standard of multiplying your dog's age by seven isn't quite accurate. Log onto **DogChannel.com/Club-Bulldog** and click on "downloads."

the Bulldog standard. Both dogs had deep chests, incredible muscle tone, roach backs (a curved spine), and low-set tails. Crib was a brindle-and-white dog that was considered to be "the best ever" for his day. He was a multi-purpose dog that was used as both a guard dog and as a family companion.

James Hinks is credited with being one of the first Bulldog exhibitors. He actively showed Bulldogs for four years, from 1860 to 1864. One of the first shows that Hinks participated in was held at the Birmingham Agricultural Hall. The show attracted an entry of forty Bulldogs including the famous red dog King Dick who was owned by Jacob Lamphier. King Dick had a very successful show career and was the first show champion and the first Bulldog to be registered in the English Kennel Club stud book. The first British Bulldog club was organized in 1864 by R.S. Rockstro.

Most of the Bulldog stock was exported to America, and the United Kingdom had the most influence on the breed's development in the United States. The first dog to be exhibited in America was "Donald," who

Wouldn't you know that the Bulldog comes from a refined pedigree?

In Savannah, Georgia, residents revere and celebrate tradition, especially on the football field.

Since 1956, a pure white English Bulldog, clad in a red sweater with a black embroidered "G" on its chest and a spiked leather collar, marches onto the football field and other sporting events as the official mascot of the University of Georgia.

From one generation to the next, each Bulldog mascot bears the name, Uga (the initials of the University of Georgia). Each comes from the same line of Bulldogs owned by Frank W. "Sonny" Seiler, a local attorney and ardent Georgia fan.

The tradition began when Seiler, a law student at Georgia, and his bride, Cecelia, were given a white Bulldog puppy as a wedding gift at a time when the campus was without a mascot. In preparation for the 1956 season opening football game, Cecelia had purchased a child's red T-shirt and sewed a black felt "G" on the chest. The newlyweds brought their T-shirt-clad Bulldog puppy to the game. Cheering in the stands with their happy, yapping Bulldog, the Seilers quickly drew the attention of fans and university officials.

So began the mascot tradition for this line of Ugas blessed with many years of football victories and famous achievements. Their accomplishments are depicted in a book, *The Real Story of Uga, the University of Georgia's Bulldog Mascots,* co-authored by Seiler and Kent Hannon. The book features 300 photos and pages of insights into the lives of six Georgia mascots on and off the field.

In its April 28, 1997, issue, *Sports Illustrated* named Uga as "the nation's best college mascot!"

it's a Fact

Before the first UGA came on the scene, two unrelated Bulldogs, Butch (1947-1950) and Mike (1951-1955), served as the University of Georgia's mascots.

photo of UGA courtesy of the University of Georgia

In the past century, Bulldogs have become considerably sounder and healthier overall. After the introduction of a distemper vaccine in the 1930s, more dogs survived puppyhood, which allowed breeders a better chance to use the best animals in the litter.

was shown in New York in 1880. He was a brindle-and-white dog owned by Sir William Verner.

Like several other breeds, the ill effects of World War I and World War II took their toll on the Bulldog. At the beginning of World War I, there were approximately 12,000 Bulldogs in the United Kingdom. By World War II, dog shows had completely ceased, and the Bulldog population decreased to 8,000. Some influential kennels of this time included Merstham, Pearson, and Cloverleys. Mrs. Pearson, of Pearson Westall's kennel, became the first lady president of the English Bulldog Club in 1936.

After World War II, many new important faces emerged that greatly influenced the breed. Jack and Kathleen Cook were credited with breeding the most U.K. Bulldog champions. Les and Ellen Cotton of the Aldridge Kennels were responsible for breeding Eng. Ch. Aldridge Advent Gold. This dog went on to sire nine U.K. champions. Other influential dogs that made their presence known were Eng. Ch. Maelor Solorium, Eng. Ch. Prince of Woodgate, and Eng. Ch. Noways Chuckley. "Chuckles" was the first Bulldog to go on to win Supreme Champion at Crufts in 1952.

The Bulldog is credited with being one of the first breeds registered with the American Kennel Club.

U.S. AND THE BULLDOG

Just as the Bulldog has enjoyed a long and colorful history of companionship in its homeland, Britain, this remarkable breed has also been embraced by Americans. Sources reveal that Bulldogs were in the United States since the moment of its inception (around 1776 or earlier). The breed was counted among the first breeds recognized by the American Kennel Club, and participated in the first Westminster Kennel Club show in 1877, where ten Bulldogs were exhibited. The first AKC champion of the breed was Robinson Crusoe, who earned the title in 1888. His brother, Britomartis, also a champion, was considered to be another fabulous specimen in the day.

Established in 1890, the Bulldog Club of America was incorporated in New York on Feb. 29, 1904. The first specialty show was held in 1907, under the auspices of the AKC. The official newsletter is called *The Bulldogger* and is available to all club members. More information about the club can be found online by visiting the website, www.thebca.org.

In the early days of the BCA, the breed was only represented at the major shows by small numbers, perhaps as few as ten dogs. The formation of the new parent club served

The Bulldog has been the breed of choice among many important people, including Winston Churchill.

to organize its members, and breeders more consistently participated in the shows. At the 1891 Westminster Kennel Club show, some fifty-one Bulldogs participated, in part due to the sixteen silver trophies and medals the BCA offered to the winners. For the next few years, the breed became a major force at

---

NOTABLE & QUOTABLE

Because there is so much local club interest in the Bulldog, good specimens can be found in all parts of the country. This has never been a boom-or-bust breed in terms of popularity, and competition for majors has always been tough. Consequently, quality has historically been quite high.

—*Bulldog breeder and judge Anne M. Hier of East Lansing, Mich.*

During World War I, Bulldogs became associated with the U.S. Marines. A Marine Corp recruiting poster of the time showed a Dachshund wearing a spiked helmet and a German Iron Cross running from a Bulldog wearing a helmet with a globe and anchor insignia. The early Marine Bulldogs were known as "Jiggs," and one starred in a 1926 movie *Tell It To the Marines.* Now the breed is the official Marine mascot, with each Marine Bulldog over the years being known as Chesty.

Modern-day Bulldogs are friendly and lovable family pets.

shows all across the United States. The Grand Trophy, originally called the Parke Cup, was the most prestigious of the awards, and the first such victor was Harper, a recent English import who caused a great stir on the American dog scene. The brindle Ch. Saleni was another Bulldog who won grandly on both sides of the Atlantic. Another great brindle English import was Ch. His Lordship, who along with Ch. Lord Yarmouth, Facey Romford, and Glenwood Queen, won consistently at dog shows during the turn of the century. His Lordship won the first two national specialties in 1894 and 1895, with Ch. Saleni taking Best of Show both years. Yarmouth won Best of Breed at the national in 1897.

Richard Croker, owner of the famed Deal Kennels, imported Ch. Rodney Stone in 1901. This highly valuable dog (said to be worth $5,000, a dear sum for a dog today, no less in 1901!) won the Grand Trophy twice (1905 and 1906) as well as the national specialty in 1901. Other top winners from this early period were Ch. La Roche, Glenwood Queen, and Alex Stewart's Strathway Prince Albert, the first Bulldog to win the Westminster show in 1913.

During the 1920s, Bulldogs were most successful, led by such kennels as Silvent White, Warleigh, Sparrow Bush, Ther-E-Aults, and Ricelands. The 1930s marked the beginning of the legacy of Edna Glass and her remarkable Bulldogs that would win for decades in the ring, including such champions as Sandow's Smasher, Sugarlite's Baby Doll, Ashford Superb, Dwael's Smasherjoe, Cherokee Morgan, and others. Dorothy Whipple-Sutcliff began her Charl-Doro Kennels in 1935 and became a force for many decades.

Charles G. Hopton, a noted Bulldog man from this period, produced many champions under his Rodney prefix, including the aptly named

Ch. L'Ambassadeur, the first Bulldog bred in the United States to win a Kennel Club championship in the United Kingdom.

The only other Bulldog to win the prestigious Westminster show was Ch. Kippax Fearnought in 1955. The dog was owned by Dr. John A. and Billie Saylor and bred by Bill Lawlor and Harold Dooler. Vardona Kennels produced the great Ch. Vardona Frosty Snowman, who became the American-bred Best in Show winner in 1959. From 1958 to 1960, Snowman won the national specialty.

From 1960 on, there have been hundreds of breeders who have made a mark on the breed in the United States, far too many to list here, but two are deserving of mention. Bob and Jean Hetherington, who have been breeding Bulldogs since 1964

under the Hetherbull prefix, have produced over 100 champions and obedience titlists, including no fewer than fourteen top producers, including the top-winning Bulldog of all time, Ch. Hetherbull Bounty's Frigate. Mrs. Hetherington earned the distinction of placing the first Utility Dog title on a Bulldog in the 1970s.

Most of the top-winning dogs and accomplished Bulldog kennels have originated from English descent. In recent years, several new faces have emerged in the Bulldog show ring in America and England. Many reputable breeders are producing quality stock and establishing reputable bloodlines. Several have done exceptionally well both in and out of the show ring.

CHAPTER 3

YOU!

D o you enjoy treasure hunts? Looking for something special and valuable that's not in plain view, but well worth the search? That's what it can be like when you find a Bulldog puppy. Where to begin? Here's your first clue: Smart owners know that the best place to find a healthy Bulldog pup is with a reputable Bulldog breeder. You may ask: Why not pick up the newspaper and read the classified section for ads or just go to a pet store?

The short answer is that buying from a reputable breeder gives you the best chance of getting a Bulldog of sound mind, body, and temperament. These people know Bulldogs. They love them, they understand them, and they want what's best for the breed as a whole and each pup they bring into the world. Breedings are carefully arranged with one purpose in mind—to better the breed.

LOOKING FOR GOLD BULLY-ION

How do buyers locate reputable Bulldog breeders? Prospective Bulldog owners can contact the Bulldog Club of America breeder referral program or a local Bulldog club. The BCA website (www.thebca.org) is a great source of information for contacting individuals and Bulldog clubs in the buyer's area.

Did You Know?

When selecting an individual puppy, keep in mind that because the Bulldog is considered a self-assured, dominant breed, the most dominant pup in a litter is generally not a good choice for a family—nor is a timid or shy puppy.

If you're in the market for a Bulldog, it is strongly advised that you contact a known breeder or a local Bulldog club.

Reputable breeders rarely advertise in newspapers; they don't need to because they usually have waiting lists for pups. Bulldog enthusiasts strongly encourage buyers to contact the national club or a local club for a list of breeders. Listed breeders usually must meet certain criteria and be willing to abide by specific standards. Dog shows are another way to locate good breeders. Check the BCA's list of shows throughout the country and visit a local Bulldog specialty (single-breed) show when it comes to town. Find somebody who shows and breeds Bulldogs. Those are the best people to go to. You're going to get quality, you're going to get health, you're going to get temperament—these folks are very cautious of what they're breeding.

Old-fashioned word of mouth is another way to learn about a reputable Bulldog breeder in your area. Ask your vet or Bulldog-owning friend for the name of a breeder they recommend.

Additionally, the Internet can be a source for finding breeders, but use caution. Many reputable breeders have websites, but not all Bulldog websites are hosted by someone who is reputable. It is not difficult to locate a reputable breeder, but it does require some homework, evaluation, logic, patience, and good judgment on the part of the buyer.

Signs of a Good Breeder
When you visit a breeder, be on the lookout for:
- a clean, well-maintained facility
- no overwhelming odors
- overall impression of cleanliness
- socialized dogs and puppies

Be ready to ask and answer a lot of questions while you search for the right Bully for your family.

SELECTING THE BEST BULLDOG BREEDER

Once you've found a few Bulldog breeders in your area, your next step is to choose one. The person you buy from is really important because you're choosing someone you'll have a relationship with for many years to come.

Call and interview several breeders. Ask how long they've been involved with Bulldogs, and why. Find out their current involvement with the breed: Are they showing? Are they club officers or rescue volunteers? Ask for the names and phone numbers of people who have bought dogs, then call those people and ask what they think about the breeder and his dogs. Find out the name of the vet who treats the breeder's dogs and call and ask the vet's opinion of the breeder and his dogs. Ask the breeder if he offers a guarantee and contract, and ask about health problems in

NOTABLE & QUOTABLE

Bulldogs are like two-year-old children their entire lives. They will continue playing with toys well into old age.

—*Stefanie Light, Bulldog rescue coordinator from Baltimore, Md.*

Picking the right Bulldog pup means finding a balance between a bossy puppy and a timid one.

the breed. Make an appointment to visit the breeder to take a look at the dogs (even if puppies aren't currently available) and their environment.

The reason for all this effort is that you need to find a trustworthy mentor—a knowledgeable, ethical person you're comfortable with and can communicate with for several years. This is especially true if you're a first-time dog owner. The first year of raising your Bulldog pup will be challenging. You want to choose a Bulldog breeder who will be helpful, as well as friendly.

Look for a person who breeds for soundness of the animals, and who breeds to better the breed. A reputable breeder also will stand behind you after the sale. You get a wealth of information from a good breeder whom you can count on as long as your dog is alive.

If you've located a reputable breeder, chances are, he will ask you plenty of questions, too. Bulldog breeders are extremely particular about who buys their pups. They want to make sure their pups go to the best homes, and will go to great lengths to ensure just that.

it's a Fact

On average, a female Bulldog whelps between four to six puppies per litter.

THE INDIVIDUAL PICK

There you are, face to face with a litter of adorable Bulldog puppies. How are you ever going to choose just one to take home? Sometimes, you won't be able to make the choice. The breeder often will match puppies and owners, based on what he knows about the puppy and about you. (Remember all those questions he asked you?) Or, one or two pups may be sold as show prospects only, rather than pets, and the breeder wants to place them in a home that will show them. The goal is to give each puppy the best home, and give each owner the puppy of his dreams. Breeders usually have a good sense of which pup goes well with which owner. If the breeder is experienced and ethical, you can relax and trust his judgment.

Even if the breeder allows you to choose a puppy, it's helpful to ask his opinion. After all,

the breeder has been in close contact with the pups since birth and knows their individual personalities. It's impossible to know as much about the litter in a few short visits. But never allow yourself to be pressured into buying a particular pup if he doesn't click with you. You always have the option to shop around or wait for another litter.

Choose a Bulldog pup who is friendly, outgoing, looks healthy, and shows no signs of aggression. Be familiar with the American Kennel Club's breed standard so you can compare the pups. Look at the puppy's size, bone density, ears, tailset, wrinkles, and color in relation to the standard. Watch the puppies interact and ask to see the parents.

Don't be in a hurry to pick your pup. Think it through. Make sure that you don't jump at the first Bulldog puppy you see.

Q&A for Owners
Be prepared for the breeder to ask you some questions.

1. Have you previously owned a Bulldog?
The breeder is trying to gauge how familiar you are with the breed. If you have never owned one, illustrate your knowledge of Bulldogs by telling the breeder about your research.

2. How many hours are you away from home during the week?
Bulldogs need lots of attention. They are not dogs who can just live in the backyard by themselves. The breeder is trying to see if you have enough time to spend

each day with your new best friend, because there aren't many things sadder than a lonely Bulldog.

3. How long have you wanted a Bulldog?
This helps a breeder know if this purchase is an impulse buy, or a carefully thought-out decision. Buying on impulse is one of the biggest mistakes owners can make. Getting a Bulldog puppy is not as quick as downloading the latest iTunes song. Be patient. It may take a week to find the right dog, or even a year. It really depends on timing.

Join Club Bulldog to get a complete list of questions a breeder should ask you. Click on "downloads" at **DogChannel.com/Club-Bulldog**

First things first: When you bring your pup home, get him to a vet.

YOUR BEST VET

As soon as you buy your puppy, make an appointment with a vet. Ask him to examine the pup for signs of ill health. Pups should not be sold before eight weeks of age, and many breeders do not sell litters until puppies are twelve to sixteen weeks old. Pups should be weaned, dewormed, and have at least the first set of vaccinations before going to new homes.

If you get as far as choosing a puppy from a litter, you will become well aware of how expensive Bulldog pups are. According to enthusiasts, these costs are due, in part, to the high cost of raising a litter of puppies; females are artificially inseminated, and whelping is by Caesarean section. Litters also can be small, and reported newborn Bulldog mortality is higher than in other breeds. You should also be aware that even if you locate a reputable Bully breeder, pups may not be available at that time. Be patient. Good things come to those who wait.

ESSENTIAL PAPERWORK

Make sure the breeder has proper papers to go with the puppy of your choice.

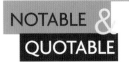

NOTABLE & QUOTABLE

Ethical breeders care about where their puppies will live. They usually want to meet the buyers and interview them, and will refuse the sale if, in the breeder's opinion, the new home is not suitable for the breed. Some breeders want to visit the prospective buyer's home before finalizing the sale.—Philip Booker, breeder in Phoenix, Az.

Are you looking for a pet who will worship the ground you walk on?

Rescue volunteers suggest that people peel their eyes away from those appealing, tempting puppies, and consider adopting an older Bulldog who's four, five, or six years old or even older.

Sometimes, a Bulldog finds himself without a home. Perhaps the owner decides he can't or won't put in the time needed to care for the dog, or can't figure out how to train him. Such a dog may be surrendered to a Bulldog rescue group, which then works to find him a new and hopefully permanent home.

These groups sometimes have young puppies available for adoption, and often have older puppies or ado-lescents. To find a Bulldog rescue group, log onto the Bulldog Club of America's website at http://thebca.org/Bulldog%20Rescue.html

There are plenty of benefits to adopting a rescued Bulldog. Such dogs have passed the chewing stage, have learned basic bathroom man-ners—and still have many years left. In addition, many rescue volunteers believe that the older dog realizes he's been saved, and repays his savior by showing lots of love and devotion.

Another way to find a Bulldog puppy who needs a new home is to log onto a national pet adoption website such as Petfinder.com (www.petfinder.com). The site's searchable database enables you to find a Bully puppy in your area who needs a break in the form of a com-passionate owner like you.

WHY NOT RESCUE?

CONTRACT: You should receive a copy of the purchase contract you signed when you bought your Bulldog puppy. The contract should specify the purchase price, health guarantee, spay/neuter requirements by a certain age, and conditions to return the pup if you find you can't keep him for any reason.

REGISTRATION PAPERS: If the breeder said that the puppy's parents were registered with the American Kennel Club or United Kennel Club, you should receive an application form to register your puppy— or at the very least, a signed bill of sale that you can use to register the puppy. The bill of sale should include the puppy's breed, date of birth, sex, registered names of the parents, litter number, the breeder's name, date of sale, and the seller's signature. Registration allows your puppy to compete in kennel club-sanctioned events such as agility and obedience trials. Registration fees support research and other activities sponsored by the organization. If your intention is to show your Bulldog, be sure not to purchase a puppy that the breeder promises is "AKC registration eligible" because it's unlikely he will be; only fully registered dogs can participate in AKC conformation shows.

PEDIGREE: The breeder should include a copy of your puppy's family tree, listing your puppy's parents, grandparents, great-grandparents, and beyond, depending on how many generations the pedigree includes. It also lists any degrees and/or titles that those relatives have earned. Look for indications that the dog's ancestors were active, successful achievers in various areas of dog sports. The information that a pedigree provides can help you understand more about the physical conformation and/or behavioral accomplishments of your Bulldog puppy's family. Usually the quality of the pedigree dictates the price of the puppy, so expect to pay a higher price for a higher quality puppy. However, chances are that you will be rewarded by the quality of life that you and your pedigreed puppy will enjoy!

JOIN OUR ONLINE **Bulldog Club**

Breeder Q&A

Here are some questions you should ask a breeder, and the preferred answers you want.

Q. How often do you have litters available?
A. The answer you want to hear is "once or twice a year" or "occasionally," because a breeder who doesn't have litters all that often is probably more concerned with the quality of his puppies, rather than with producing a lot of puppies to make money.

Q. What is the goal of your breeding program?
A. A good answer is "to improve the breed" or "to breed for temperament."

Q. What kinds of health problems have you had with your Bulldogs?
A. Beware of a breeder who says, "none." Every breed has health issues.

Get a complete list of questions and answers at Club Bulldog. Log onto **DogChannel.com/Club-Bulldog** and click on "downloads."

Pedigree is very crucial with this breed, so make sure you get a family tree chart from your breeder.

The Bulldog was originally developed to be a fighter, not a lover! Female Bulldogs typically require artificial insemination to get pregnant. Natural mating can be possible for the breed, but it is very difficult.

HEALTH RECORDS: You should receive a copy of your puppy's health records, including his date of birth, visits to the vet, and immunizations. Bring the health records to your veterinarian when you take your puppy in for his first checkup, which should take place within a few days of his arrival in your household. The records will become part of your puppy's permanent health file.

CARE INSTRUCTIONS: The breeder should provide written instructions on basic puppy care, including when and how much to feed him.

GETTING READY

Knowing how to find a reputable breeder is essential to getting a healthy and sound Bulldog. But enthusiasts say it's also important that smart prospective owners be prepared to raise a puppy. You need a lot of patience with a puppy. Don't expect to leave a puppy to grow up into an obedient, good-natured adult

A healthy puppy should have a moist snout; a shiny, soft coat; and a lot of energy.

if you leave him alone for nine hours a day. You must have time and patience with puppies.

Demands aside, life with a Bulldog is a treasure trove, enthusiasts say. Be prepared to enjoy a great friendship with your Bully and the possibility of a high-maintenance companion. Whatever the cost, a relationship with a Bulldog is priceless.

Did You Know?

Bulldogs were not made for birthing. Most Bulldog puppies are born by Caesarean section. Free-whelping can and does occur occasionally, but it is not the norm. The Bulldog's large head and narrow hips make a natural birth very difficult.

Signs of a Healthy Puppy

Here are a few things you should look for when selecting a puppy.

1. **NOSE:** It should be slightly moist to the touch, but there shouldn't be excessive discharge. The puppy should not be sneezing or sniffling persistently.

2. **SKIN AND COAT:** The puppy's coat should be soft and shiny, without flakes or excessive shedding. Watch out for patches of missing hair, redness, bumps, or sores. The pup should have a pleasant smell. Check for parasites, such as fleas or ticks.

3. **BEHAVIOR:** A healthy puppy may be sleepy, but should not be lethargic. A healthy pup will be playful at times, not isolated in a corner. You should see occasional bursts of energy and interaction with littermates. When it's mealtime, a healthy pup will take an interest in his food.

There are more signs to look for when picking out the perfect Bulldog puppy. Download the list at **DogChannel.com/Club-Bulldog**

Researching a dog breed and finding a breeder are only two aspects of the "homework" a smart owner will have to do before bringing a Bulldog puppy home. You will also have to prepare your home and family for the new addition. Much as you would prepare a nursery for a newborn baby, you will need to designate a place in your home that will be the puppy's own. How you prepare your home will depend on how much freedom the dog will be allowed. Whatever you decide, you must ensure that your Bulldog has a place that he can call his own.

When you bring your new puppy into your home, you are bringing him into what will become his home, as well. Obviously, you did not buy a puppy so that he could run your household, but in order for a puppy to grow into a stable, well-adjusted dog, he has to feel comfortable in his surroundings. Their natural curiosity can border on recklessness, which means puppy-proofing your humble abode from the ground up.

How you prepare your home will depend on how much freedom the dog will be allowed. In the case of your Bulldog,

it's a Fact

Dangers lurk indoors and out. Keep your curious Bulldog from investigating your shed and garage. Antifreeze and fertilizers, such as those you would use for roses, will kill a Bulldog. Keep these items on high shelves that are out of reach for your low-sniffing Bully.

designating a couple of rooms for the puppy is ideal.

In order for a Bulldog puppy to grow into a stable, well-adjusted dog, he has to feel comfortable in his surroundings. Remember, he is leaving the warmth and security of his mother and littermates, as well as the familiarity of the only place he has ever known, so it is important to make his transition to your home—his new home—as easy as possible.

PUPPY-PROOFING

Aside from making sure that your Bulldog will be comfortable in your home, you also

have to make sure that your home is safe, which means taking the proper precautions to keep your pup away from things that are dangerous for him.

Puppy-proof your home inside and out. Place breakables out of reach. If he is limited to certain places within the house, keep potentially dangerous items in off-limit areas. If your Bulldog is going to spend

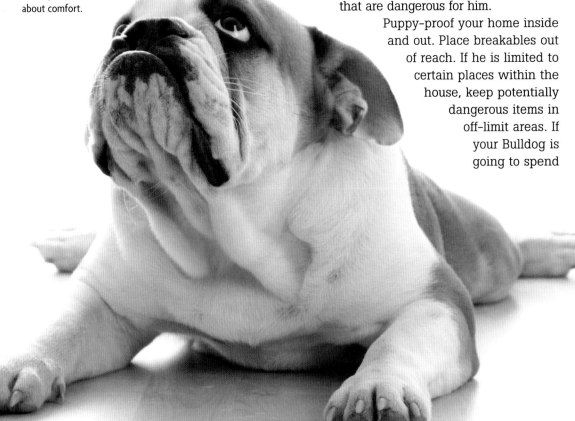

Bulldogs are all about comfort.

time in a crate, make sure that there is nothing near his crate that he can reach if he sticks his curious little nose or paws through the openings.

The outside of your home must also be safe for your pup. Your puppy will naturally want to run and explore the yard, and he should be granted that freedom—as long as you are there to supervise him. Do not let a fence give you a false sense of security; you would be surprised how crafty (and persistent) a dog can be in figuring out how to dig under a fence or squeeze his way through holes. The remedy is to make the fence well embedded into the ground. Be sure to repair or secure any gaps in the fence. Check the fence periodically to ensure that it is in good shape and make repairs as needed; a very determined pup may work on the same spot until he is able to get through.

The following are a few common problem areas to watch out for in the home.

Electrical cords and wiring: No electrical cord or wiring is safe. Office-supply stores sell products to keep wires gathered under computer desks, as well as products that prevent office chair wheels (and puppy teeth) from damaging electrical cords. If you have exposed cords and wires, these products aren't very expensive and can be used to keep a pup out of trouble.

Trash cans: Don't waste your time trying to train your Bulldog not to get into the trash. Simply put the trash or garbage

SMART TIP!

A well-stocked toy box should contain three main categories of toys:
1. **action** (anything that you can throw or roll and get things moving)
2. **distraction** (durable toys that make dogs work for a treat)
3. **comfort** (soft, stuffed little "security blankets")

Bulldogs are masters at getting into things, so be sure your stuff is put away.

behind a cabinet door and use a child-safe lock if necessary. Be aware that dogs love bathroom trash (i.e., cotton balls, cotton swabs, used razors, dental floss, etc.), which consists of items that are all extremely dangerous! Put this trash can in a cabinet under the sink and make sure you always shut the door to the bathroom.

Household cleaners: Make sure your Bulldog puppy doesn't have access to any of these deadly chemicals. Keep them behind closed cabinet doors, using child-safe locks if necessary.

Pest control sprays and poisons: Chemicals to control ants or other pests should never be used in the house, if possi-

Puppy-proofing your house should begin even before your Bulldog puppy comes home for the fist time.

NOTABLE & QUOTABLE

The first thing you should always do before your puppy comes home is to lie on the ground and look around. You want to be able to see everything your puppy is going to see. For the puppy, the world is one big chew toy.—Cathleen Stamm, rescue volunteer in San Diego, Calif.

9-1-1! If you don't know whether the plant or food or "stuff" your Bulldog just ate is toxic to dogs, you can call the ASPCA's Animal Poison Control Center (888-426-4435). Be prepared to provide your puppy's age and weight, his symptoms—if any—and how much of the plant, chemical, or substance the puppy ingested, as well as how long ago you think he came into contact with the substance. The ASPCA charges a consultation fee for this service.

ble. Your puppy doesn't have to directly ingest these poisons to become ill; if your Bulldog steps in the poison, he can experience toxic effects by licking his paws. Roach motels and other poisonous pest traps are also evidently yummy to dogs, so don't drop these poisons behind couches or cabinets; it's quite possible that if there's room for a roach motel, there's room for a determined Bulldog.

Fabric: Here's one you might not think about: Some puppies have a habit of licking blankets, upholstery, rugs, or carpets. Though this habit seems fairly innocuous, over time the fibers from the upholstery or carpet can accumulate in the dog's stomach and cause a blockage. If you see your dog licking any of these items, remove the item or prevent your Bulldog from having contact with it.

Prescriptions, painkillers, supplements and vitamins: Keeping medications on a counter or the kitchen table isn't safe. All medications should be kept in a high cabinet. Also, be very careful when taking your prescription medications, supplements, or vitamins: How often have you

Don't let your Bulldog make a habit of licking fabrics. The ingested fibers could cause intestinal damage.

Keep your puppy's first day home low-key, so as not to scare him.

dropped a pill? With a Bulldog, you can be assured that your puppy will be in between your legs and will snarf up the pill before you can even start to say "No!" Dispense your pills carefully and without your Bulldog present.

Miscellaneous loose items: If it's not bolted to the floor, your puppy is likely to give the item a taste test. Socks, coins, children's toys, game pieces, cat bell balls—you name it; if it's on the floor, it's worth a try. Make sure the floors in your home are picked up and free of clutter.

FAMILY INTRODUCTIONS

Everyone in the house will be excited about the puppy's homecoming and will want to pet him and play with him, but it is best to make the introduction low-key so as not to overwhelm the puppy. He is apprehensive already. It is the first time he has been separated from his mother, littermates, and the breeder. The ride to your home is likely the first time he has been in a car. The last thing you want to do is smother your Bulldog, as this will only frighten him further. This is not to say that human contact is not extremely necessary at this stage, because this is the time when a connection between the pup and his human family is formed. Gentle petting and soothing words should help console your Bulldog, as well as just putting him down and letting him explore on his own (under your watchful eye, of course).

Your pup may approach the family members or may busy himself with exploring the house for a while. Gradually, each person should spend some time with the pup, one at a time, crouching down to get as close to the dog's level as possible and letting him sniff their hands before petting him gently. He definitely needs human attention, and he needs to be touched; this is how to form an immediate bond. Just remember that the pup is experiencing a lot of things for the first time, at the same time. There are new people, new noises, new smells, and new things to investigate, so be gentle, be affectionate, and be as comforting as you can be.

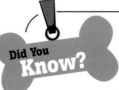

Did You Know?

Everyone who rides in your car has to buckle up—even your Bulldog! Your dog can travel in the car inside his crate, or you can use a doggie seat belt. These look like harnesses that attach to your car's seat-belt system.

PUP'S FIRST NIGHT HOME

You have traveled home with your new charge safely in his crate. He may have already been to the vet for a thorough checkup, he's been weighed, his papers examined; perhaps he's even been vaccinated and wormed, as well. Your Bulldog has met and licked the whole family, including the excited children and the less-than-happy cat. He's explored his area, his new bed, the

Your teething puppy will need lots of chew toys to help him through the pain—but not the baby's toys! Get your Bully his own things to gnaw on.

Playing with toys from puppyhood encourages good behavior and social skills throughout the dog's life. A happy, playful dog is a content and well-adjusted one. Also, because all puppies chew to soothe their gums and help loosen puppy teeth, they should always have easy access to several different toys.—dog trainer and author Harrison Forbes of Savannah, Tenn.

yard, and anywhere else he's permitted. He's eaten his first meal at home and relieved himself in the proper place. Your Bulldog has heard lots of new sounds, smelled new friends, and seen more of the outside world than ever before.

This was just the first day! He's worn out and is ready for bed—or so you think! Remember, this is your puppy's first night to sleep alone. His mother and littermates are no longer at paw's length, and he's scared, cold, and lonely. Be reassuring to your new family member. This is not the time to spoil your Bulldog and give in to his inevitable whining.

Puppies whine. They whine to let others know where they are and hopefully to get company out of it. Place your pup in his new bed or crate in his room and close the door. Mercifully, he may fall asleep without a peep. If the inevitable occurs, ignore the

Funny Bone

Q. How do you turn a fox into a Bulldog?
A. You marry her!

whining; he is fine. Do not give in and visit your pup. He will fall asleep eventually.

Many breeders recommend placing a piece of bedding from his former home in his new bed so that he recognizes the scent of his littermates. Others still advise placing a hot water bottle in his bed for warmth. The latter may be a good idea provided the pup doesn't attempt to suckle; he'll get good and wet and may not fall asleep as fast.

Place food and water bowls in the same place to set up a routine.

A sturdy collar and leash are musts for dog walks and training.

Your puppy should look upon his crate as a welcome refuge, like a den. Feed him in it, and put suitably safe bedding inside for his frequent naps. Also, confine your dog within the crate at regular intervals, allowing him to become comfortable with this sometimes-necessary restriction.

Your Bulldog's first night can be stressful for him and his new family. Remember that you are setting the tone of nighttime at your house. Unless you want to play with your pup every night at 10 p.m., midnight, and 2 a.m., don't initiate the habit. Your family will thank you, and so will your pup!

SHOPPING FOR A BULLDOG

It's fun shopping for a new puppy. From training to feeding and sleeping to playing, your new Bulldog will need a few items to make life comfy, easy, and fun. Be prepared and visit your local pet-supply store before you bring home your new family member.

Collar and ID tag: Accustom your dog to wearing a collar the first day you bring him home. Not only will a collar and ID tag help your pup in the event that he becomes lost, but collars are also an important training tool. If your Bulldog gets into trouble, the collar will act as a handle, helping you divert her to a more appropriate behavior. Make sure the collar fits snugly enough so that your Bulldog cannot wriggle out of it, but is loose enough so that it will not be uncomfortably tight around his neck. You should be able to fit a finger between your pup and the collar. Collars come in many styles, but for starting out, a simple buckle collar with an easy-release snap works great.

Leash: For training or just for taking a stroll down the street, a leash is your Bulldog's vehicle to explore the outside world. Like collars, leashes come in a variety of styles and

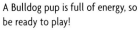
A Bulldog pup is full of energy, so be ready to play!

materials. A 6-foot nylon leash is a popular choice because it is lightweight and durable. As your pup grows and gets used to walking on the leash, you may want to purchase a flexible leash. These leads allow you to extend the length to give your dog a broader area to explore or to shorten the length to keep him closer to you.

Bowls: Your Bulldog will need two bowls: one for water and one for food. You may want two sets of bowls, one for inside and one for outside, depending on where your dog will be fed and where he will be spending time. Bowls should be sturdy enough so that they don't tip over easily. (Most have reinforced bottoms that prevent tipping.) Bowls are commonly made out of metal, ceramic, or plastic, and should be easy to clean.

Crate: A crate is multipurpose. It serves as a bed, house-training tool, and travel carrier. It also is the ideal doggie den—a bedroom of sorts—that your Bulldog can retire to when he wants to rest or just needs a break. The crate should be large enough for your Bulldog to stand in, turn around, and lie down. You don't want any more room than this—especially if you're planning on using the crate to house-train your dog—because he will eliminate in one corner and lie down in another. Get a crate that is big enough for your dog when he is an adult. Then use dividers to limit the space when he's a puppy.

Bed: A plush doggie bed will make sleeping and resting more comfortable for your Bulldog. Dog beds come in all shapes, sizes, and colors, but your dog just needs one that is soft and large enough for him to stretch out on. Because puppies and rescue dogs often don't come house-trained, it's helpful to buy a bed that can be washed easily. If your Bulldog will be sleeping in a crate, a nice crate pad and a small blanket that he can "burrow" in will help him feel more at home. Replace the blanket if it becomes ragged and starts to fall apart because your Bulldog's nails could get caught in it.

Gate: Similar to those used for toddlers, gates help keep your Bulldog confined to one room or area when you can't supervise him. Gates also work to keep your dog out of areas you don't want him in. Gates are available in many styles.

Toys: Keep your dog occupied and entertained by providing him with an array of fun toys. Teething puppies like to chew— in fact, chewing is a physical need for pups as they are teething—and everything from your shoes to the leather couch to the Oriental rug are fair game. Divert your Bulldog's chewing instincts with durable toys like bones made of nylon or hard rub-

Preparing your home for your new dog will help him feel loved.

ber. Other fun toys include rope toys, treat-dispensing toys, and balls. Make sure the toys and bones don't have any small parts that could break off and be swallowed, causing your dog to choke. Stuffed toys are popular, but they can become destuffed, and an overly excited puppy may ingest the stuffing or the squeaker. Check your Bulldog's toys regularly and replace them if they become frayed or show signs of wear.

Cleaning supplies: Until your Bulldog puppy is reliably house-trained, you will be doing a lot of cleaning. Accidents will occur, which is acceptable in the begin-

it's a **Fact**

Correctly socializing your puppy requires that you provide gentle guidance, positive feedback, and ongoing excursions into new worlds before she reaches adulthood.

ning because your puppy won't know any better. All you can do is be prepared to clean up any accidents. Old rags, towels, newspapers, and a stain and odor remover are good to have on hand. Don't scold your Bulldog puppy for a puddle either. The mistake was made by you; you didn't supervise him closely enough to see his potty signs.

BEYOND THE BASICS

These items are the bare necessities. You will find out what else you need as you go along—grooming supplies, flea/tick protection, etc. It will vary depending on your situation, but it is important that you have everything you need to feed and make your Bulldog comfortable during his first few days at his new home.

JOIN OUR ONLINE **Bulldog Club**

Some ordinary household items make great toys for your Bulldog—as long you make sure they are safe. You will find a list of homemade toys at **DogChannel.com/Club-Bulldog**

HOUSE-TRAINING

Unexciting as it may be, the house-training part of puppy rearing greatly affects the budding relationship between a smart owner and his Bulldog puppy—particularly when it becomes an area of ongoing contention. Fortunately, armed with suitable knowledge, patience, and common sense, you'll find house-training progresses at a relatively smooth rate. That leaves more time for the important things, like cuddling your adorable puppy, showing him off, and laughing at his numerous antics.

The answer to successful house-training is total supervision and management—crates, tethers, exercise pens, and leashes—until you know your dog has developed substrate preferences for outside surfaces (grass, gravel, concrete) instead of carpet, tile, or hardwood, and knows that potty happens outside.

IN THE BEGINNING

For the first two to three weeks of a puppy's life, his mother helps the pup to eliminate. The mother also keeps the whelping box or "nest area" clean. When pups begin to walk around and eat on their own,

it's a Fact

Ongoing house-training difficulties may indicate that your Bulldog puppy has a health problem, warranting a veterinary checkup. A urinary infection, parasites, a virus, and other nasty issues greatly affect your puppy's ability to hold pee or poop.

they choose where they eliminate. You can train your puppy to relieve himself wherever you choose, but this must be somewhere suitable. You should bear in mind from the outset that when your puppy is old enough to go out in public places, any canine deposits must be removed at once. You will always have to carry with you a small plastic bag or "poop-scoop."

Outdoor training includes such surfaces as grass, soil, and concrete. Indoor training usually means training your dog on newspaper. When deciding on the surface and location that you will want your Bulldog to use, be sure it is going to be permanent. Training your dog on grass and then changing two months later is extremely difficult for dog and owner.

Next, choose the command you will use each and every time you want your puppy to void. "Let's go," "hurry up," and "potty" are examples of commands commonly used by smart dog owners.

Get in the habit of giving your puppy the chosen relief cue before you take him out. That way, when he becomes an adult, you will be able to determine if he wants to go out when you ask him. A confirmation will be signs of interest, such as wagging his tail, watching you intently, going to the door, etc.

LET'S START WITH THE CRATE

Clean animals by nature, dogs keenly dislike soiling where they sleep

A gate is useful to train your dog indoors.

and eat. This fact makes a crate a useful tool for house-training. When purchasing a new crate, consider that one correctly sized will allow adequate room for an adult dog to stand full-height, lie on his side without scrunching, and turn around easily. If debating plastic versus wire crates, short-haired breeds sometimes prefer the warmer, draft-blocking quality of plastic, while furry dogs often like the cooling airflow of a wire crate.

Some crates come equipped with a movable wall that reduces the interior size to provide enough space for your puppy to stand, turn, and lie down, while not allowing room to soil one end and sleep in the other. The problem is that if your puppy goes potty in the crate anyway, the divider forces him to lie in his own excrement.

This can work against you by desensitizing your puppy against his normal, instinctive revulsion to resting where he's elimi-

Did You Know?

Cleaning accidents properly with an enzyme solution will dramatically reduce the time it takes to house-train your dog because he won't be drawn back to the same areas.

nated. If scheduling permits you or a responsible family member to clean the crate soon after it's soiled, then you can continue to crate-train because limiting crate size does encourage your puppy to hold it. Otherwise, give him enough room to move away from an unclean area until he's better able to control his elimination.

Needless to say, not every Bulldog puppy adheres to this guideline. If your puppy moves along at a faster pace, thank your lucky stars. Should he progress slower, accept it and remind yourself that he'll improve. Be aware that pups frequently hold it longer at night than during the day. Just because your puppy sleeps for six or more hours through the night, it does not mean he can hold it that long during the more active daytime hours.

One last bit of advice on the crate: Place it in the corner of a normally trafficked room, such as the family room or kitchen. Social and curious by nature, dogs like to feel included in family happenings. Creating a quiet retreat by putting the crate in an unused area may seem like a good idea, but results in your puppy feeling insecure and isolated. Watching his people pop in and out of the crate room reassures your puppy that he's not forgotten.

PUPPY'S NEEDS

Your puppy needs to relieve himself after play periods, after each meal, after he has been sleeping, and any time he indicates that he is looking for a place to urinate or defecate.

When you take your Bulldog outside to potty, make sure it is all business first. He can play after he completes his "transaction."

The urinary and intestinal tract muscles of very young puppies are not fully developed. Therefore, like human babies, puppies need to relieve themselves frequently. Take your Bulldog puppy out often—every hour for an eight-week-old, for example—and always immediately after sleeping and eating. The older the puppy, the less often he will need to relieve himself. Finally, as a mature, healthy adult, he will require only three to five relief trips per day.

HOUSING HELPS

Because the types of housing and control you provide for your Bulldog puppy have a direct relationship on the success of housetraining, you must consider the various aspects of both before beginning training. Taking a new puppy home and turning him loose in your house can be compared to turning a child loose in a sports arena and telling the child that the place is all his! The sheer enormity of the place would be too

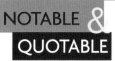

NOTABLE &
QUOTABLE

Reward your pup with a high-value treat immediately after he potties to reinforce going in the proper location, then play for a short time afterward. This teaches that good things happen after pottying outside!—Victoria Schade, certified pet dog trainer, from Annandale, Va.

much for him to handle. Instead, offer the puppy clearly defined areas where he can play, sleep, eat, and live. A room of the house where the family gathers is the most obvious choice. Puppies are social animals and need to feel like they are a part of the pack right from the start. Hearing your voice, watching you while you are doing things, and smelling you nearby are all positive reinforcers that he is now a member of your pack. Usually a family room, the kitchen or a nearby adjoining breakfast area is ideal for providing safety and security for puppy and owner.

Within that room, there should be a smaller area that your Bulldog puppy can call his own. An alcove, a wire or fiberglass dog crate, or a fenced (not boarded!) corner from which he can view the activities of his new family will be fine. The size of the area or crate is the key factor here. The area must be large enough for the puppy to lie down and stretch out his body, yet small enough so that he cannot relieve himself at one end and sleep at the other without coming into contact with his droppings before he is fully trained to relieve himself outside.

Dogs are, by nature, clean animals and will not remain close to their relief areas unless forced to do so. In those cases, they then become dirty dogs and usually remain that way for life.

The designated area should be lined with clean bedding and a toy. Water must always be available, in a nonspill container, once the dog is house-trained reliably.

True Tails

One aspect of house-training that catches most folks by surprise relates to how often that little puppy must potty.

Trainer and Bulldog fancier Theresa Crowley, who lives in Malvern, Pa., says helping an eight- or nine-week-old Bulldog avoid eliminating indoors requires hourly outside trips. He may not "go" each outing, but up to twenty times is quite possible.

Alas, busy lives mean few owners enjoy the luxury of taking their puppies outside every hour. So, savvy Bulldoggers do the next best thing and provide an indoor arrangement that allows your Bulldog to maintain the natural canine instinct to eliminate away from where he sleeps and eats, thus promoting clean habits.

To do this, set up a crate or X-pen (exercise pen) arrangement. Though a smaller crate better encourages your puppy to eliminate outside her bed, most dogs quickly accept an adult-sized crate as their special area. This means one large enough that a full-grown Bulldog will be able to stand, turn around, and lie flat in.

Plastic crates prove less drafty; wire crates provide better airflow. Because you know your Bulldog cannot tolerate heat or cold and you plan to keep him in a temperature-controlled environment, the type of crate your get falls to personal preference. For wire, inch-square spacing will stop your pup's feet from going through the openings while he rolls around, avoiding possible injury.

X-pens are usually roofless, foldable wire or plastic confinements that shape into a square or circular enclosure. Crowley recommends one 3-feet tall to discourage an ambitious puppy from climbing out. Better yet, purchase a "topper" for extra insurance. Clips designed like leash snaps secure the X-pen together, and a door made into the pen allows easy access for getting your dog in and out.

Your puppy should look upon the crate as a welcome refuge, like a den. Feed him in it, and put suitably safe bedding inside for his frequent naps. Also, allow him to become comfortable with this sometimes-necessary restriction.

House-training a Bully requires some patience.

IN CONTROL

By control, we mean helping the puppy to create a lifestyle pattern that will be compatible to that of his human pack (you!). Just as we guide children to learn our way of life, we must show our pup when it is time to play, eat, sleep, exercise, and entertain himself.

Your Bulldog puppy should always sleep in his crate. He should also learn that, during times of household confusion and excessive human activity, such as at breakfast when family members are preparing for the day, he can play by himself in relative safety and comfort in his designated area. Each time you leave your Bulldog alone, he should understand exactly where he is to stay.

Puppies are chewers. They cannot tell the difference between lamp cords, television wires, shoes, or table legs. Chewing into a television wire, for example, can be

SMART TIP!

When distance prevents you from going home at lunch or during periods when overtime crops up, make alternative arrangements for getting your puppy out. Hire a pet-sitting or walking service, or enlist the aid of an obliging neighbor to help.

fatal to the Bulldog puppy, while a shorted wire can start a fire in the house.

If the puppy chews on the arm of the chair when he is alone, you probably will discipline him angrily when you get home. Thus, he makes the association that your coming home means he is going to be punished. (He will not remember chewing the chair and is incapable of making the association of the discipline with his naughty deed.)

Other times of excitement, such as family parties, can be fun for your puppy, provided that he can view the activities from the security of his designated area. He is not underfoot, and he is not being fed all

Putting your pup on an eating and potty schedule will help you out, too!

sorts of tidbits that will probably cause him stomach distress, yet he still feels a part of the fun.

SCHEDULE A SOLUTION

A puppy should be taken to his relief area each time he is released from his designated area, after meals, after play sessions, and when he first awakens in the morning (at age eight weeks, this can mean 5 a.m.!). The puppy will indicate that he's ready "to go" by circling or sniffing busily—do not misinterpret these signs. For a puppy less than ten weeks of age, a routine of taking him out every hour is necessary. As the puppy grows, he will be able to wait for longer periods of time.

Keep trips to your Bulldog puppy's relief area short. Stay no more than five or six minutes, and then return to the house. If he goes during that time, praise him lavishly and take him indoors immediately. If he does not, but he has an accident when you go back indoors, pick him up immediately, say "No! No!" and return to his relief area. Wait a few minutes, then return to the house again. Never hit your Bulldog puppy or rub his face in urine or excrement when he has had an accident.

Once indoors, put your puppy in his crate until you have had time to clean up his accident. Then release him to the family area and watch him more closely than before. Chances are, his accident was a result of your not picking up his potty signals or waiting too long before offering him the opportunity to relieve himself. Never hold a grudge against your Bulldog puppy for accidents.

Let the puppy learn that going outdoors means it is time to relieve himself, not to play. Once trained, he will be able to play indoors and out and still differentiate between the times for play versus the times for relief.

Help him develop regular hours for naps, being alone, playing by himself, and just resting, all in his crate. Encourage him to entertain himself while you are busy elsewhere. Let him learn that having you nearby is comforting, but it is not your main purpose in life to provide him with undivided attention.

Each time you put a puppy in his own area, use the same command, whatever suits you best. Soon he will run to his crate or special area when he hears you say those words.

Remember that one of the primary ingredients in house-training your puppy is control. Regardless of your lifestyle, there will always be occasions when you will need to have a place where your dog can stay and be happy and safe. Crate-training is the answer for now and in the future.

A few key elements are really all you need for a successful house-training method—consistency, frequency, praise, control, and supervision. By following these procedures with a normal, healthy puppy, you and your Bulldog will soon be past the stage of accidents and ready to move on to a full and rewarding life together.

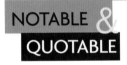

Having housetraining problems with your Bulldog?
Ask other Bully owners for advice and tips. Log onto
DogChannel.com/Club-Bulldog and click on "community."

EVERYDAY CARE

Your selection of a veterinarian should be based his skills with dogs, and, if possible, especially Bulldogs. If the vet is based nearby, it will be helpful because you might have an emergency or need to make multiple visits for treatments.

FIRST STEP: SELECT THE RIGHT VET

All licensed veterinarians are capable of dealing with routine medical issues such as infections and injuries, and the promotion of health (for example, by vaccination). If the problem affecting your Bulldog is more complex, your veterinarian will refer your pet to a specialist like a veterinary dermatologist, veterinary ophthalmologist, etc., whatever field you require.

Veterinary procedures are very costly and, as the treatments available improve, they are going to become more expensive. It is quite acceptable to discuss matters of cost with your vet; if there is more than one treatment option, cost may be a factor in deciding which route to take.

To begin, look for a veterinarian before you actually need one. Smart owners ideally start looking for a veterinarian a month or two before they bring home their new Bulldog puppy. That will give you time to meet candidate veterinarians, check out the condition of the clinic, and see who you feel comfortable with. If you already have a pet, look sooner rather than later, preferably not in the midst of a veterinary health crisis.

Second, define the criteria that are important to you. Points to consider or investigate:

● **Convenience.** Proximity to your home, extended hours, or drop-off services are helpful for people who work regular business hours, have a busy schedule or don't want to drive far. If you have mobility issues, finding a veterinarian who makes house calls or a service that provides pet transport might be particularly important.

● **Size.** A one-person practice ensures that you'll always be dealing with the same veterinarian during each and every visit. "That person can really get to know you and your dog," says Bernadine Cruz, D.V.M., of Laguna Hills Animal Hospital in California. The downside, though, is that the sole practitioner does not have the immediate input of another veterinarian, and if your veterinarian becomes ill or takes time off, you are out of luck.

The multiple-doctor practice offers consistency if your pet needs to come in unexpectedly on a day when your veterinarian isn't there. Additionally, your vet can quickly consult with his colleagues within the clinic if he is unsure about a diagnosis or treatment.

If you find a veterinarian within that practice who you really like, you can make your appointments with that individual, establishing the same kind of bond that you would with the solo practitioner.

● **Appointment Policies.** Some veterinary practices operate strictly by appointment only, which may minimize your wait time. However, if a sudden problem arises with your Bulldog and the vets are booked up, they might not be able to squeeze your pet in that day. Some clinics are drop-in only—great for impromptu or crisis visits, but without scheduling could involve longer waits to see the next available vet—whoever is open, not someone in particular. Some veterinary practices maintain an appointment schedule but also keep slots open throughout the day for walk-in visitors, offering the best of both worlds.

● **Basic vs. State-of-the-Art vs. Full-Service.** A practice with high-tech equipment offers greater diagnostic capabilities and treatment options, important for tricky or difficult cases. However, the cost of pricey equipment gets passed along to the

Picking the right vet is one of the most important decisions you'll make for the lifelong health of your new family member. Make sure you ask the right questions to ensure that your vet is knowledgeable not only about dogs, but Bulldogs in particular. Download a list of questions to ask potential vets by logging on to **DogChannel.com/Club-Bulldog**—just click on "downloads."

client, so you could pay a little more for routine procedures—the bulk of most pets' appointments. Some practices offer boarding, grooming, training classes, and other services right on the premises, conveniences some pet owners appreciate.

● **Fees and Payment Polices.** How much is a routine office visit? If there's a significant price difference, ask why. If you have health insurance for your Bulldog or want to pay by credit card, make sure the candidate clinic accepts those payment options.

FIRST VET VISIT

It is much easier, less costly, and more effective to practice preventive medicine than to fight bouts of illness and disease.

When selecting a vet, look for one with experience with Bulldogs.

Properly bred puppies of all breeds come from parents who were selected based on their genetic disease profile. The puppies' mother should have been vaccinated, free of all internal and external parasites, and properly nourished. For these reasons, a visit to the veterinarian who cared for the dam (mother) is recommended if at all possible. The dam passes disease resistance to her puppies, which should last from eight to ten weeks. Unfortunately, she also can pass on parasites and infection. This is why knowledge about her health is useful in learning more about the health of the puppies.

Now that your Bulldog puppy is home safe and sound, it's time to arrange your pup's first trip to the veterinarian. Perhaps the breeder can recommend someone in the area who specializes in Bulldogs, or maybe you know some Bulldog owners who can suggest a good vet. Either way, you should make an appointment within a couple of days of bringing home your Bulldog. If possible, see if you can stop for this first vet appointment before going home.

The pup's first vet visit will consist of an overall examination to make sure that the pup does not have any problems that are not apparent to you. The veterinarian also will set up a schedule for the pup's vaccinations; the breeder will inform you of which ones the pup has already received, and the vet can continue from there.

The puppy also will have his teeth examined and have his skeletal conformation and general health checked prior to certification by the veterinarian. Puppies in certain breeds have problems with their kneecaps, cataracts and other eye problems, heart murmurs, and undescended testicles. They may also have personality problems, and your veterinarian might have training in temperament evaluation.

VACCINATION SCHEDULING

Most vaccinations are given by injection and should only be given by a veterinarian. Both you and the vet should keep a record of the date of the injection, the identification of the vaccine, and the amount given. Some vets give a first vaccination at eight weeks of age, but most dog breeders prefer the course not to commence until about ten weeks because of interaction with the antibodies produced by the mother. The vaccination scheduling is usually based on a fifteen–day cycle. You must take your vet's advice as to when to vaccinate, as this may differ according to the vaccine used.

The usual vaccines contain immunizing doses of several different viruses such as distemper, parvovirus, parainfluenza, and hepatitis. There are other vaccines available when the puppy is at risk. You should rely on professional advice. This is especially true for the booster immunizations. Most vaccination programs require a booster when the puppy is a year old and once a year thereafter. In some cases, circumstances may require more frequent immunizations.

Kennel cough, more formally known as tracheobronchitis, is immunized against with a vaccine that is sprayed into the dog's nostrils. Kennel cough is usually included in routine vaccinations, but it is often not as effective as the vaccines for other major diseases.

Your veterinarian probably will recommend that your puppy be fully vaccinated before you bring him outside. There are airborne diseases, parasite eggs in the grass, and unexpected visits from other dogs that might be dangerous to your puppy's health. Other dogs are the most harmful reservoir of pathogenic organisms, as everything they have can be transmitted to your puppy.

Five Months to One Year of Age: Unless you intend to breed or show your dog, neutering the puppy at six months of age is recommended. Discuss this with your veterinarian. Neutering/spaying has proven to be beneficial to male and female puppies, respectively. Besides eliminating the possibility of pregnancy, it inhibits (but does not prevent) breast cancer in females and prostate cancer in male dogs.

Your veterinarian should provide your Bulldog puppy with a thorough dental evaluation at six months of age, ascertaining whether all his permanent teeth have

The first order of business is getting your puppy's shots.

erupted properly. A home dental care regimen should be initiated at six months, including weekly brushing and providing good dental devices (such as nylon bones). Regular dental care promotes healthy teeth, fresh breath, and a longer life.

Dogs Older Than One Year: Continue to visit the veterinarian at least once a year. There is no such disease as "old age," but bodily functions do change with age. The eyes and ears are no longer as efficient. Liver, kidney, and intestinal functions often decline. Proper dietary changes, recommended by your veterinarian, can make life more pleasant for your aging Bulldog and you.

EVERYDAY HAPPENINGS

Keeping your Bulldog healthy is a matter of keen observation and quick action when necessary. Knowing what's normal for your dog will help you recognize signs of trouble before they blossom into a full-blown emergency situation.

Even if the problem is minor, such as a cut or scrape, you'll want to care for it immediately to prevent subsequent infections, as well as to ensure that your dog doesn't make it worse by chewing or scratching at it. Here's what to do for common, minor injuries or illnesses, and how to recognize and deal with emergencies.

Cuts and Scrapes: For a cut or scrape that is half an inch or smaller, clean the wound with saline solution or warm water and use tweezers to remove any debris. Apply antibiotic cream. No bandage is necessary unless the wound is on a paw, which can pick up dirt when your dog walks on it. Deep cuts with lots of bleeding or those caused by sharp objects should be treated by your vet.

Cold Symptoms: Dogs don't actually get colds, but they can get illnesses that have similar symptoms, such as coughing, a runny nose, or sneezing. Dogs cough for any number of reasons, from respiratory infections to inhaled irritants to congestive heart failure. Take your Bulldog to the vet for prolonged coughing, or coughing accompanied by labored breathing, runny eyes or nose, or bloody phlegm.

A runny nose that continues for more than several hours requires veterinary attention, as well. If your Bulldog sneezes, he may have some mild nasal irritation that will resolve on its own, but frequent sneezing, especially if it's accompanied by a runny nose, may indicate anything from allergies to an infection to something stuck in the nose.

Vomiting and Diarrhea: Sometimes dogs suffer minor gastric upsets when they eat a new type of food, eat too much, eat the contents of the trash can, or become excited or anxious. Give your Bulldog's stomach a rest by withholding food for twelve hours, and then feeding him a bland diet such as baby food or rice and chicken, gradually returning your Bulldog to his normal food. Projectile vomiting, or vomiting or diarrhea that continues for more than forty-eight hours, is another matter. If this happens, take your Bulldog to the veterinarian.

HEAT AND THE BULLDOG

Many dog breeds love the heat; Bulldogs aren't one of them. As is often the case with

NOTABLE & QUOTABLE

If you have a Bulldog with a deep nose wrinkle, it will swell and get infected if it's not kept clean.

—breeder Darlene Stuedemann of Clinton, Iowa

Always be on the lookout for unusual behavior in your Bulldog.

VET VISITS AND EVERYDAY CARE | 83

Heat can cause your Bulldog distress, so keep him cool and wet to beat the heat.

brachycephalic dogs, Bulldogs are at increased risk of overheating (hyperthermia), a dangerous condition if not treated quickly. Hyperthermia can cause seizures, brain and other internal damage, collapse, coma, and even death. Use the following tips to avoid heat stress.

◆ Keep your dog in air-conditioning during hot, humid weather.

◆ Make sure your Bulldog always has access to cool, shady areas and fresh water.

◆ Avoid activities during the heat of the day, limiting exercise and play times to early morning or late evening when it's cooler.

◆ Monitor outside play and exercise so your dog doesn't overexert himself, reducing the length and intensity of exercise during hot spells.

◆ Douse your dog with a little cool water or wet towels while he's exercising, and wash or spritz his feet with cool water if he starts to get hot.

Signs of overheating and overexercising include rapid breathing or heavy panting. If your dog seems to be struggling for air, passes out, or his tongue starts to turn blue, seek emergency treatment immediately.

BULLDOG ON A DIET

Obesity is the most common canine nutrition-related health problem. An obese dog weighs twenty percent more than his ideal weight. Symptoms and effects of obesity include development of diseases such as diabetes, liver disease, pancreatitis, and hip dysplasia. Decreased exercise capacity

JOIN OUR ONLINE
Bulldog Club

Just like with infants, puppies need a series of vaccinations to ensure that they stay healthy during their first year of life. Download a vaccination chart from **DogChannel.com/Club-Bulldog** that you can fill out for your baby Bully.

makes it more likely that the weight problem will continue.

To prevent your Bulldog from gaining weight, feed regular meals (instead of free-choice) with limited, low-calorie treats. Make sure your furry friend exercises daily, even if it's just walking (if your dog has health problems, ask your veterinarian to recommend a suitable exercise program).

If your Bully does get hefty, consult your veterinarian about a weight-loss plan for your dog, which should include a complete checkup, as well as dietary and exercise recommendations. Dogs with severe obesity may benefit from dirlotapide (Slentrol), an oral medication that blocks fat absorption.

Obesity is common in Bulldogs, so keep yours on a healthy diet.

SENIOR BULLDOGS

For dogs, as well as their masters, old is relative. Certainly we can distinguish between a Bulldog puppy and an adult Bulldog—there are the obvious physical traits—such as size, appearance, and facial expressions—and personality traits. Puppies and young dogs like to play with children. Children's natural exuberance is a good match for the seemingly endless energy of young dogs. They like to run, jump, chase and retrieve. When dogs grow up and cease their interaction with children, they are often thought of as being too old to play with the kids. On the other hand, if a Bulldog is only exposed to people with less active lifestyles, his life will normally be less active, and he will not seem to be getting old as his activity level slows down.

If people live to be 100 years old, dogs live to be twenty years old. When trying to compare dog years to human years, you cannot make a generalization about all dogs. You can make the generalization that eight to ten years is a good lifespan for a Bulldog, although some Bulldogs have been known to live to fifteen years. Dogs are generally considered mature within three years, but they can reproduce even earlier. So the first three years of a dog's life are like seven times that of comparable humans. That means a three-year-old dog is like a twenty-one-year-old human. As the curve of comparison shows, there is no hard and fast rule for comparing dog and human ages. The comparison is made even more difficult, because not all humans age at the same rate. And females tend to live longer than males.

Most veterinarians and behaviorists use the seven-year mark as the time to consider a dog a senior. The term senior does not imply that the dog is geriatric and has begun to fail in mind and body. Aging is essentially a slowing process. Humans readily admit that they feel a difference in their activity level from age twenty to thirty, and then from thirty to forty, etc. By treating the seven-year-old dog as a senior, owners are able to implement certain therapeutic and preventive medical strategies with the help of their veterinarians.

A senior-care program should include at least two vet visits per year, screening sessions to determine the dog's health status, as well as nutritional counseling. Veterinarians determine the senior dog's health status through a blood smear for a complete blood count, serum chemistry profile with electrolytes, urinalysis, blood pressure check, electrocardiogram, ocular tonometry (pressure on the eyeball), and dental prophylaxis.

Such an extensive program for senior dogs is well advised before smart owners start to see the obvious physical signs of aging, such as slower and inhibited movement, graying, increased sleep/nap periods, and disinterest in play and other activity. This preventive program promises a longer, healthier life for the aging dog. Among the physical problems common in aging dogs are the loss of sight and hearing, arthritis, kidney and liver failure, diabetes mellitus, heart disease, and Cushing's disease (a hormonal disease).

In addition to the physical manifestations discussed, there are also some behavioral changes and problems related to aging dogs. Dogs suffering from hearing or vision loss, dental discomfort, or arthritis can become aggressive. Likewise the near-deaf and/or blind dog may be startled more easily and react in an unexpectedly aggressive manner. Seniors suffering from senility can become more impatient and irritable. Housesoiling accidents are associated with loss of mobility, kidney problems and loss of sphincter control as well as plaque accumulation, physiological brain changes and reactions to medications. Older dogs, just like young puppies, suffer from separation anxiety, which can lead to excessive barking, whining, housesoiling, and destructive behavior. Seniors may become fearful of everyday sounds, such as vacuum cleaners, heaters, thunder, and passing traffic. Some dogs have difficulty sleeping, due to discomfort, the need for frequent toilet visits and the like.

Owners should avoid spoiling the older Bulldog with too many fatty treats. Obesity is a common problem in older dogs and subtracts years from their lives. Keep the senior Bully as trim as possible because excessive weight puts additional stress on the body's vital organs. Some breeders recommend supplementing the diet with foods high in fiber and lower in calories. Adding fresh vegetables and marrow broth to the senior's diet makes a tasty, low-calorie, low-fat supplement. Vets also offer specialty diets for senior dogs that are worth exploring.

NOTABLE & QUOTABLE *The most common allergic triggers are environmental allergens, including house dust mites and pollens, and food allergen, most commonly beef, corn, soy, and chicken. Fleas also are known to worsen flares. Skin bacteria and skin yeast can also be the cause of an allergic reaction, or they can secondarily infect pre-existing allergic skin lesions.*

—Thierry Olivry, associate professor of dermatology at North Carolina State University

Proper nutrition and sufficient exercise are good health measures to prevent disease.

Your dog, as he nears his twilight years, needs his owner's patience and good care more than ever. Never punish an older dog for an accident or abnormal behavior. For all the years of love, protection, and companionship that your dog has provided, he deserves special attention and courtesies. The older dog may need to relieve himself at 3 a.m. because he can no longer hold it for eight hours. Older dogs may not be able to remain crated for more than two or three hours. It may be time to give up a sofa or chair to your old friend. Although he may not seem as enthusiastic about your attention and petting, he does appreciate the considerations you offer as he gets older.

Your Bulldog does not understand why his world is slowing down. Smart owners must make the transition into the golden years as pleasant and rewarding as possible.

No matter how careful you are with your darling Bully, sometimes unexpected injuries happen. Be prepared for any emergency by creating a canine first-aid kit. Find out what essentials you need on **DogChannel.com/Club-Bulldog**—click on "downloads."

JOIN OUR ONLINE Bulldog Club

L ike any purebred dog, Bulldogs have their share of breed-specific health problems. That said, breeders and other Bulldog lovers are ready to counter any claims that this breed has more health problems than most.

SKIN PROBLEMS

Veterinarians are consulted by dog owners about skin problems more than for any other group of diseases or maladies. A dog's skin is as sensitive, if not more so, as human skin, and both suffer almost the same ailments.

Because many skin problems have visual symptoms that are almost identical, it requires the skill of an experienced veterinary dermatologist to identify and cure many of the more severe skin disorders. Pet-supply stores sell many treatments for skin problems, but most of them are directed at symptoms and not at the underlying problem(s). If your Bulldog is suffering from a skin disorder, seek professional assistance as quickly as possible. As with all diseases, the earlier a problem is identified and treated, the more likely the cure will be successful. There are active programs being undertaken by many veterinary pharmaceutical manufacturers to solve most, if not all, of the common skin problems in dogs.

it's a
Fact

Dogs can get Lyme disease, Rocky Mountain spotted fever, tick bite paralysis, and many other diseases from ticks.

PARASITE BITES

Insect bites itch, erupt, and may even become infected. Dogs have the same reaction to fleas, ticks, and/or mites. When an insect lands on you, you have the chance to whisk it away with your hand. Unfortunately, when a Bulldog is bitten by a flea, tick, or mite, he can only scratch it away or bite it. By the time your Bulldog has been bitten, the parasite has done its damage. It may also have laid eggs, which will cause further problems in the future. The itching from parasite bites is probably due to the saliva injected into the site when the parasite sucks the dog's blood.

AUTO-IMMUNE ILLNESS

An auto-immune illness is one in which the immune system overacts and does not recognize parts of the affected person. Instead, the immune system starts to react as if these parts were foreign and need to be destroyed. An example is rheumatoid arthritis, which occurs when the body does not recognize the joints, which leads to a very painful and damaging reaction in the joints. This has nothing to do with age, so it can occur in puppies. The wear-and-tear arthritis in older people or dogs is called osteoarthritis.

Did You Know?

Like many other big-jowled breeds, the Bulldog has a reputation for drooling and slobbering over everything and everybody. But for the Bulldog at least, the myth of 24/7 jowl-dripping is just that: a myth. The bottom line on the wet mouth: A careful search for a reputable breeder should allow you bypass the baby bib aisle when shopping for Bulldog supplies.

Lupus is another auto-immune disease that affects dogs as well as people. It can take variable forms, affecting the kidneys, bones, and the skin. It can be fatal, so it is treated with steroids, which can themselves have very significant side effects. Steroids calm down the allergic reaction to the body's tissues, which helps the lupus, but they also calm down the body's reaction to real foreign substances such as bacteria. Steroids also thin the skin and bones.

AIRBORNE ALLERGIES

Just as humans suffer from hay fever during the pollinating season, many dogs suffer from the same allergies. When the pollen count is high, your dog might suffer, but don't expect him to sneeze or have a runny nose like a human. Dogs react to pollen allergies in the same way they react to fleas; they scratch and bite themselves. Dogs, like humans, can be tested for allergens. Discuss the testing with your veterinarian.

FOOD ALLERGIES

Feeding your dog properly is very important. An incorrect diet could affect your Bulldog's health, behavior, and nervous system, possibly making a normal dog an aggressive one. The result of a good—or bad—diet is most visible in a dog's skin and coat, but internal organs are affected, too.

Dogs are allergic to many foods that are popular and highly recommended by breeders and veterinarians. Changing the brand of food may not eliminate the problem if the ingredient to which your dog is allergic is contained in the new brand.

Recognizing an allergy can be difficult. Humans often have rashes or swelling of the lips or eyes when they eat foods they are allergic to. Dogs do not usually develop rashes, but they react the same way they do to an airborne or bite allergy—they itch, scratch, and bite. While pollen allergies and parasite bites are usually seasonal, food allergies are year-round problems.

Diagnosis of a food allergy is based on a two- to four-week dietary trial with a home-cooked diet fed to the exclusion of all other foods. The diet should consist of boiled rice or potato with a source of protein that the dog has never eaten before, such as fresh or frozen fish, lamb, or even something as exotic as pheasant.

Water has to be the only drink, and it is important that no other foods are fed during this trial. If your dog's condition improves, try the original diet again to see if the itching resumes. If it does, then your dog is allergic to his original diet. You must find a diet that does not distress your dog's skin. Start with a commercially available hypoallergenic diet or the homemade diet that you created for the allergy trial.

Food intolerance is the dog's inability to completely digest certain foods. This occurs because he does not have the chemicals (enzymes) necessary to digest some food. All puppies have the enzymes necessary to digest canine milk, but some do not have the

If food allergies are getting your dog down, try asking the vet about options.

enzymes to digest cow milk, resulting in loose bowels, stomach pains, and gas.

Dogs often do not have the enzymes to digest soy or other beans. The treatment is to exclude these foods from your Bulldog's diet.

EXTERNAL PARASITES

Fleas: Of all the problems to which dogs are prone, none is better known and more frustrating than fleas. Flea infestation is relatively simple to cure but difficult to prevent.

To control flea infestation, you have to understand the flea's life cycle. Fleas are often thought of as a summertime problem, but centrally heated homes have made fleas a year-round problem. The most effective method of flea control is a two-stage approach: Kill the adult fleas, then control the development of pre-adult fleas. Unfortunately, no single active ingredient is effective against all stages of the flea life cycle.

Treating fleas should be a two-pronged attack. First, the environment needs to be treated; this includes carpets and furniture, especially the dog's bedding and areas underneath furniture. The environment should be treated with a household spray containing an insect growth regulator and an insecticide to kill the adult fleas. Most IGRs are effective against eggs and larvae; they actually mimic the fleas' own hormones and stop the eggs and larvae from developing into adult fleas. There are currently no treatments available to attack the pupae stage of the life cycle, so the adult insecticide is used to kill the newly hatched adult fleas

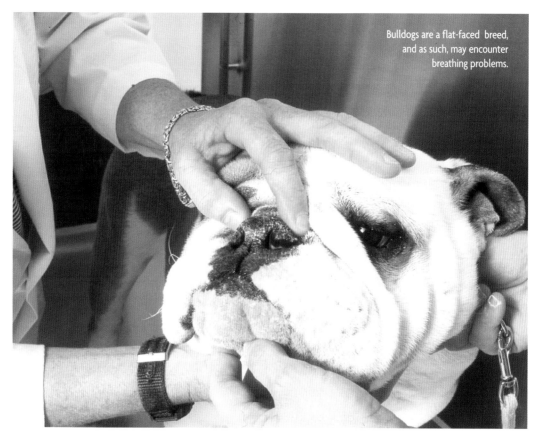

Bulldogs are a flat-faced breed, and as such, may encounter breathing problems.

before they find a host. Most IGRs are active for many months, while adult insecticides are only active for a few days.

When treating with a household spray, vacuum before applying the product. This stimulates as many pupae as possible to hatch into adult fleas. The vacuum cleaner should also be treated with an insecticide to prevent the eggs and larvae that have been collected in the vacuum bag from hatching.

The second treatment stage is to apply an adult insecticide to the dog. Traditionally, this would be in the form of a collar or a spray, but more recent innovations include digestible insecticides that poison the fleas when they ingest the dog's blood. Alternatively, there are drops that, when placed on the back of the dog's neck, spread throughout the hair and skin to kill adult fleas.

Ticks: Though not as common as fleas, ticks are found all over the tropical and temperate world. They don't bite like fleas; they harpoon. They dig their sharp proboscis (nose) into the dog's skin and drink the blood, which is their only food and drink. Ticks are controlled the same way fleas are controlled.

The American dog tick, *Dermacentor variabilis*, may well be the most common dog tick in many geographical areas, especially in hot and humid areas. Most dog ticks have life expectancies of a week to six months, depending on climatic conditions. They can neither jump nor fly, but they can crawl slowly and can range up to

Did You Know? Across the globe, more than 800 species of ticks exist, and they aren't particular to where they dine. Mammals, birds, and reptiles are all fair game.

sixteen feet to reach a sleeping or unsuspecting Bulldog.

Mites: Just as fleas and ticks can be problematic for your dog, mites can also lead to an itch fit. Microscopic in size, mites are related to ticks and generally take up permanent residence on their host animal—in this case, your dog! The term "mange" refers to any infestation caused by one of the mighty mites, of which there are six varieties that smart dog owners should know.

● *Demodex mites* cause demodicosis (sometimes called "red mange" or "follicular mange"), a condition in which the mites live in the dog's hair follicles and sebaceous glands in larger-than-normal numbers. Most dogs recover from this type of mange without any treatment, though topical therapies are commonly prescribed by the vet.

● The *Cheyletiellosis mite* is the hook-mouthed culprit associated with walking dandruff, a condition that affects dogs as well as cats and rabbits. If untreated, this mange can affect a whole kennel of dogs and can be spread to humans, as well.

● The *Sarcoptes mite* causes intense itching on the dog in the form of a condition known as scabies or sarcoptic mange. Scabies is highly contagious and can be passed to humans. Sometimes an allergic reaction to the mite worsens the severe itching associated with sarcoptic mange.

● Ear mites, *Otodectes cynotis*, lead to otodectic mange, which commonly affects the outer ear canal of the dog, though other areas can be affected as well. Your vet can prescribe a treatment to flush out the ears and kill any eggs in the ears. A complete month of treatment is necessary to cure this mange.

● Two other mites, less common in dogs, include *Dermanyssus gallinae* (the "poultry" or "red mite") and *Eutrombicula alfreddugesi* (the North American mite associated with trombiculidiasis or chigger infestation). The types of mange caused by both of these mites must be treated by vets.

INTERNAL PARASITES

Most animals—fishes, birds, and mammals, including dogs and humans—have worms and other parasites that live inside their bodies. According to Dr. Herbert R. Axelrod, a fish pathologist, there are two kinds of parasites: dumb and smart. The smart parasites live in peaceful cooperation with their hosts (symbiosis), while the dumb parasites kill their hosts. Most worm infections are relatively easy to control. If they are not controlled, they weaken the host dog to the point that other

medical problems occur, but they do not kill the host as dumb parasites would.

Roundworms: Roundworms that infect dogs live in the intestines and shed eggs continually. It has been estimated that a dog produces about six or more ounces of feces every day. Each ounce averages hundreds of thousands of roundworm eggs. There are no known areas in which dogs roam that do not contain roundworm eggs. Because roundworms infect people, too, it is wise to have your dog regularly tested.

Some dogs catch external parasites like ticks just from walking through grass. Always be aware of your dog's risk.

Roundworm infection can kill puppies and cause severe problems in adult dogs, as the hatched larvae travel to the lungs and trachea through the bloodstream. Cleanliness is the best preventive for roundworms. Always pick up after your dog and dispose of feces in appropriate receptacles.

Hookworms: Hookworms are dangerous to humans as well as to dogs and cats, and can cause severe anemia due to iron deficiency. The worm uses its teeth to attach itself to the dog's intestines and changes the site of its attachment about six times per day. Each time the worm repositions itself, the dog loses blood and can become anemic.

Symptoms of hookworm infection include dark stools, weight loss, general weakness, pale coloration, and anemia, as well as possible skin problems. Fortunately, hookworms are easily purged with a number of medications that have proven effective. Discuss these with your veterinarian. Most heartworm preventives include a hookworm insecticide, as well.

In young puppies, roundworms cause bloated bellies, diarrhea, coughing, and vomiting, and are transmitted from the mother (through blood or milk). Affected puppies will not appear as animated as normal puppies. The worms appear spaghetti-like, measuring as long as 6 inches!

Humans can be infected by hookworms, too! We can acquire the larvae through exposure to contaminated feces. Because the worms cannot complete their life cycle on a human, the worms simply infest the skin and cause irritation. As a preventive, use disposable gloves or a "poop-scoop" to pick up your dog's droppings and prevent your dog (or neighborhood cats) from defecating in children's play areas.

Tapeworms: There are many species of tapeworm, all of which are carried by fleas! Fleas are so small that your Bulldog could pass them onto your hands, your plate, or your food, making it possible for you to ingest a flea that is carrying tapeworm eggs. While tapeworm infection is not life-threatening in dogs (smart parasite!), it can be the cause of a very serious liver disease in humans.

Whipworms: In North America, whipworms are counted among the most common parasitic worms in dogs. Affected dogs may only experience upset tummies, colic, and diarrhea. These worms, however, can live for months or years in the dog, beginning their larval stage in the small intestine, spending their adult stage in the large intestine and finally passing infective eggs through the

dog's feces. The only way to detect whipworms is through a fecal examination, though this is not always foolproof.

Treatment for whipworms is tricky, due to the worms' unusual life cycle, and often dogs are reinfected due to exposure to infective eggs on the ground. Cleaning up droppings in your backyard as well as in public places is absolutely essential for sanitation purposes and the health of your dog and others.

Threadworms: Though less common than roundworms, hookworms, and those previously mentioned parasites, threadworms concern dog owners in southwestern United States and the Gulf Coast area where the climate is hot and humid. Living in the small intestine of the dog, this worm measures a mere 2 millimeters and is round in shape. Like the whipworm, the threadworm's life cycle is

If your Bully is just plain dog tired all the time, he may be suffering from an illness. Take him to the vet for a thorough exam.

very complex, and the eggs and larvae are passed through the feces. A deadly disease in humans, threadworms readily infect people, most commonly through the handling of feces. Threadworms are most often seen in young puppies in the form of bloody diarrhea and pneumonia. Sick puppies must be isolated and treated immediately; vets recommend a follow-up treatment one month later.

Heartworms: Heartworms are thin, extended worms up to 12 inches long, that live in a dog's heart and the major blood vessels surrounding it. Dogs may have up to 200 heartworms. Symptoms may be loss of energy, loss of appetite, coughing, the development of a pot belly, and anemia.

Heartworms are transmitted by mosquitoes, which drink the blood of infected dogs and take in larvae with the blood. The larvae, called *microfilariae*, develop within the body of the mosquito and are passed on to the next dog bitten after the larvae mature. It takes two to three weeks for the larvae to develop to the infective stage within the body of the mosquito. Dogs are usually treated at about six weeks of age and maintained on a prophylactic dose given monthly.

Blood testing for heartworms is not necessarily indicative of how seriously your dog is infected. Although this is a dangerous disease, it is not easy for a dog to be infected. Discuss the various preventives with your vet, because there are many different types now available. Together you can decide on a safe course of prevention for your dog.

BULLDOG HEALTH DILEMMAS

Diseases of concern in Bulldogs include entropion, brachycephalic syndrome, hypothyroidism, and torn cruciate ligaments.

ENTROPION: Common in many breeds, entropion is a painful condition where the rim of the eyelid rolls inward and touches the eyeball. As a result, the eyeball retracts in the eye socket and the eyelid hairs and lashes rub against the cornea, causing irritation and damage. Entropion occurs in upper and/or lower eyelids, in one or both eyes. Ectropion is the opposite of entropion in that the eyelids turn outward, rather than in, and cause the lower lid to split.

Causes of entropion are either developmental or acquired secondarily to other eye problems. Dogs with development entropion show signs before one year of age; acquired entropion can occur at any age.

Signs of entropian can include squinting, rubbing the eyes, tearing, sometimes a thick discharge. Treatment varies according to the type of entropion and age of the Bulldog. For very mild development and acquired cases, topical lubricants can help. Secondary entropion is addressed by treating the primary cause. For developmental cases in pup-pies, temporarily tacking back the eyelid with sutures is the treatment of choice. Some Bulldog puppies eventually outgrow the entropion as their facial conformation changes. If developmental entropion persists into adulthood, permanent correction can be made by surgically removing a small slice or piece of eyelid tissue.

BRACHYCEPHALIC SYNDROME: Bulldogs are a brachycephalic breed, meaning they have flat faces and short muzzles. As such, they have the anatomical components of a regular size muzzle but in a much smaller, compressed space. The jaws develop normally in width but not in length, sometimes giving rise to physiological problems collectively known as brachycephalic syndrome.

Brachycephalic syndrome manifests as airway interference and breathing disorders. Conditions relating to this syndrome can include the following.

A good way to keep your Bully healthy is by grooming him regularly.

- stenotic nares (narrowed or constricted nostril openings)
- elongated soft palate (the palate is too long in proportion to the head, extending into the throat)
- redundant pharyngeal tissue (folds of excess tissue in the throat)
- everted laryngeal saccules (small structures on the side of the larynx are pulled out of position, into and blocking the opening into the lower airway)
- hypoplastic trachea (abnormal growth of the cartilage rings that comprise the trachea, resulting in a narrowed airway)
- collapsed larynx (breakdown of the laryngeal walls)
- heat and exercise intolerance (overheating resulting in respiratory stress)

Signs include a noisy respiratory tract—snorting, snuffling, coughing, or gagging. If your Bulldog seems to be struggling for air or passes out, or his tongue or gums start to turn blue, seek emergency treatment immediately.

Treatment depends on the condition and severity of the symptoms. In particular, keep your dog at a proper weight, avoid intense activities during hot and humid weather, and monitor your dog during exciting or stressful situations, as rapid breathing can cause airway tissues to become inflamed and swell, aggravating airway problems. Use a harness to walk or secure your Bulldog (the strain of a collar pressing onto the larynx and trachea could further stress the area). Severely affected dogs may need surgery.

While most Bulldogs do not suffer from brachycephalic syndrome, any brachycephalic dog undergoing anesthesia (for diagnosis, spay/neuter, dental exam, or surgery) should receive an examination and assessment of the palate and larynx at the same time.

HYPOTHYROIDISM: Hypothyroidism is a disease whereby the thyroid gland fails to produce adequate amounts of thyroid hormones. Although the condition is not fatal, if unchecked the disease can significantly reduce your Bulldog's quality of life, as thyroid hormones affect many different body systems. A very common disease in the general dog population, hypothyroidism usually occurs in dogs age three years or older.

Signs include unexplained weight gain; lethargy; reduced playfulness; exercise intolerance; seeking out warm places to sleep; recurrent staph, yeast, or ear infections; dull, brittle, or thinning coat; and dry or oily skin.

Often, a simple, quick, inexpensive blood test (T4 measurement) can identify the disease. Treatment is a thyroid hormone pill given once or twice daily for the rest of your Bulldog's life.

CRUCIATE LIGAMENT RUPTURE: One of the most common orthopedic injuries in dogs is a cruciate ligament rupture. As with

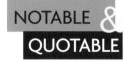

NOTABLE & QUOTABLE

Bulldogs are labeled as "walking vet bills." But Bulldogs can be healthy—very healthy, in fact. Yes, they can have health issues, but just as any breed can. I suggest doing your research, but use common sense as well. Give yourself every chance possible of getting a healthy puppy by taking your time and going to a reputable breeder.

—Nikki Bermea, a breeder from Woodbine, N.J.

humans, two cruciate ligaments cross inside the knee (stifle): The cranial or anterior (front) and the posterior (back). These ligaments help support the various structures inside the knee, and if they partially tear or completely rupture, the knee becomes unstable and arthritis sets in within a couple of weeks. In dogs, the cranial cruciate ligament is the one most commonly affected.

CLR usually occurs during some bout of activity such as running or jumping. The cause is unknown, although limb conformation and genetics may be factors.

Signs include an intermittent or chronic lameness in the rear leg ranging from mild to severe to nonweightbearing. Depending on the dog's size, activity level, and severity of injury, treatment is found in nonsurgical management or surgery plus physical therapy

Whichever surgical method is used, the keys to the most successful recovery are eight to twelve weeks of strict rest coupled with physical therapy.

Keeping your dog conditioned and in good weight means less stress on the knee and its joint, and less risk of a cruciate tear.

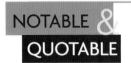

NOTABLE & QUOTABLE

If you do observe lameness in your dog, see your veterinarian sooner rather than later. If we can treat these injuries early, we may be able to increase our ability to manage them medically rather than surgically.—Robert S. Gilley, D.V.M.

Before you participate in any sports training with your Bulldog, take him to the vet to make sure he is healthy enough.

FOOD FOR

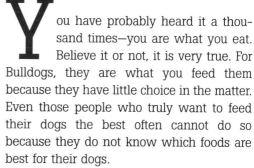

THOUGHT

You have probably heard it a thousand times—you are what you eat. Believe it or not, it is very true. For Bulldogs, they are what you feed them because they have little choice in the matter. Even those people who truly want to feed their dogs the best often cannot do so because they do not know which foods are best for their dogs.

Today the choices of food for your dog are many and varied. There are simply dozens of brands of food in all sorts of flavors and textures, ranging from puppy diets to those for seniors. There are even hypoallergenic and low-calorie diets available. Because your Bulldog's food has a bearing on coat, health, and temperament, it is essential that the most suitable diet is selected. It is fair to say, however, that even smart owners can be somewhat perplexed by the enormous range of dog foods available. Only understanding what is best for your dog will help you reach an informed decision.

BASIC TYPES

Dog foods are produced in various types: dry, wet (canned), semimoist, fresh packaged, and frozen.

it's a
Fact **Bones can cause gastrointestinal obstruction and perforation, and may be contaminated with salmonella or E. coli. Leave them in the trash and give your dog a nylon bone toy instead.**

If you're feeding a puppy food that's complete and balanced, your Bulldog youngster doesn't need any dietary supplements such as vitamins, minerals, or other types of food. Dietary supplementation could even harm your puppy by unbalancing his diet. If you have questions about supplementing your Bulldog's diet, ask your veterinarian.

Dry foods are useful for the cost-conscious because they tend to be less expensive than the others. They also contain the least fat and the most preservatives. Dry food is bulky and takes longer to eat than other foods, so it's more filling.

Wet food—available in cans or foil pouches—is usually sixty to seventy percent water and is more expensive than dry food. A palatable source of concentrated nutrition, wet food makes a good supplement for underweight dogs or those recovering from illness. Some owners add a little wet food to dry food to increase its appeal.

Semimoist food is flavorful but usually contains lots of sugar, which can lead to dental problems and obesity. It's not a good choice for your Bulldog's main diet.

Likewise, **frozen** food, which is available in cooked and raw forms, is usually more expensive than wet foods. The advantages of frozen food are similar to those of wet foods.

The amount of food your Bulldog needs depends on a number of factors, such as age, activity level, food quality, reproductive status, and size. What's the easiest way to figure it out? Start with the manufacturer's recommended amount, then adjust it according to your dog's response. For example, feed the recommended amount for a few weeks and if your Bulldog loses weight, increase the amount by ten to twenty percent. If your dog gains weight, decrease the amount. It won't take long to determine the amount of food that keeps your little friend in optimal condition.

NUTRITION 101

All Bulldogs (and all dogs, for that matter) need proteins, carbohydrates, fats, vitamins, and minerals for optimal growth and health.

■ **Proteins** are used for growth and repair of muscles, bones, and other bodily tissues. They're also used for production of antibodies, enzymes, and hormones. All dogs need protein, but it's especially important for puppies because they grow and develop so rapidly. Protein sources include various types of meat, meat meal, meat byproducts, eggs, dairy products, and soybeans.

■ **Carbohydrates** are metabolized into glucose, the body's principal energy source. Carbohydrates are available as sugars, starches, and fiber.

• Sugars (simple carbohydrates) are not suitable nutrient sources for dogs.

• Starches—a preferred type of carbohydrates in dog food—are found in a variety of plant products. Starches must be cooked in order to be digested.

• Fiber (cellulose)—also a preferred type of carbohydrate in dog food—isn't digestible but helps the digestive tract function properly.

■ **Fats** are also used for energy and play an important role in skin and coat health, hormone production, nervous system function, and vitamin transport. Fat increases the palatability and the calorie count of puppy/dog food, which can lead to serious health problems, such as obesity, for puppies or dogs that are allowed to overindulge. Some foods contain added amounts of omega fatty acids such as docosohexaenoic acid, a compound that may enhance brain development and learning in puppies but is not considered an essential nutrient by the Association

of American Feed Control Officials (www. aafco.org). Fats used in dog foods include tallow, lard, poultry fat, fish oil, and vegetable oils.

■ **Vitamins** and **minerals** help muscle and nerve functions, bone growth, healing, metabolism, and fluid balance. Especially important for your puppy are calcium, phosphorus, and vitamin D, which must be supplied in the right balance to ensure proper development of bones and teeth.

Just as your Bulldog needs proper nutrition from his food, water is an essential "nutrient" as well. Water keeps the dog's body properly hydrated and promotes normal function of the body's systems.

During house-training, it is necessary to keep an eye on how much water your Bulldog is drinking, but once he is reliably trained, he should have access to clean, fresh water at all times, especially if you feed dry food. Make sure that your Bulldog's water bowl is clean, and that you change the water often.

CHECK OUT THE LABEL

To help you get a feel for what you are feeding your dog, start by taking a look at the label on the package or can. Look for the words "complete and balanced." This tells you that the food meets specific nutritional requirements set by the AAFCO for either adults ("maintenance") or puppies and pregnant/lactating females ("growth and reproduction"). The label must state the group for which it is intended. Because you're feeding a puppy, choose a "growth and reproduction" food.

The label also includes a nutritional analysis, which lists minimum protein, minimum fat, maximum fiber, and maximum moisture content, as well as other information. (You won't find carbohydrate content because it's everything that isn't protein, fat, fiber, and moisture.)

The nutritional analysis refers to crude protein and crude fat—amounts that have been determined in the laboratory. This analysis is technically accurate, but it doesn't

Real bones are not safe snacks for dogs. A good alternative is nylon bones, which are less likely to splinter and cause choking.

Dogs of all ages love treats and table food, but these goodies can unbalance your Bulldog's diet and lead to a weight problem if you don't choose and feed them wisely. Table food, whether fed as a treat or as part of a meal, shouldn't account for more than ten percent of your Bulldog's daily caloric intake. If you plan to give your Bully treats, be sure to include "treat calories" when calculating the daily food requirement—so you don't end up with a pudgy pup!

When shopping for packaged treats, look for ones that provide complete nutrition—they're basically dog food in a fun form. Choose crunchy goodies for chewing fun and dental health. Other ideas for tasty treats include:

✓ small chunks of cooked, lean meat
✓ dry dog food morsels
✓ cheese
✓ veggies (cooked, raw or frozen)
✓ breads, crackers, or dry cereal
✓ unsalted, unbuttered, plain, popped popcorn

Some foods, however, can be dangerous and even deadly to a dog. The following items can cause digestive upset (vomiting or diarrhea) or toxic reactions that could be fatal:

✗ **avocados:** can cause gastrointestinal irritation, with vomiting and diarrhea, if eaten in sufficient quantity

✗ **baby food:** may contain onion powder; does not provide balanced nutrition

✗ **chocolate:** contains methylxanthines and theobromine, caffeine-like compounds that can cause vomiting, diarrhea, heart abnormalities, tremors, seizures, and death. Darker chocolates contain higher levels of the toxic compounds.

✗ **eggs, raw:** whites contain an enzyme that prevents uptake of biotin, a B vitamin; may contain salmonella

✗ **garlic (and related foods):** can cause gastrointestinal irritation and anemia if eaten in sufficient quantity

✗ **grapes:** can cause kidney failure if eaten in sufficient quantity (the toxic dose varies from dog to dog)

✗ **macadamia nuts:** can cause vomiting, weakness, lack of coordination, and other problems.

✗ **meat, raw:** may contain harmful bacteria such as salmonella or E. coli

✗ **milk:** can cause diarrhea in some puppies.

✗ **onions (and related foods):** can cause gastrointestinal irritation and anemia if eaten in sufficient quantity

✗ **raisins:** can cause kidney failure if eaten in sufficient quantity (the toxic dose varies from dog to dog)

✗ **yeast bread dough:** can rise in the gastrointestinal tract, causing obstruction; produces alcohol as it rises

tell you anything about digestibility: how much of the particular nutrient your Bulldog can actually use. For information about digestibility, contact the manufacturer (check the label for a telephone number and website address).

Virtually all commercial puppy foods exceed AAFCO's minimum requirements for protein and fat, the two nutrients most commonly evaluated when comparing foods. Protein levels in dry puppy foods usually range from about twenty-six to thirty percent; for canned foods, the values are about nine to thirteen percent. The fat content of dry puppy foods is about twenty percent or more; for canned foods, it's eight percent or more. (Dry food values are larger than canned food values because

dry food contains less water; the values are actually similar when compared on a dry matter basis.)

Finally, the label lists the food's ingredients in descending order by weight. Manufacturers are allowed to list separately different forms of a single ingredient (e.g., ground corn and corn gluten meal). The food may contain things like meat byproducts, meat and bone meal, and animal fat, which probably won't appeal to you but are nutritious and safe for your Bulldog puppy. Higher quality foods usually have meat or meat products near the top of the ingredient list, but you don't need to worry about grain products as long as the label indicates that the food is nutritionally complete. Dogs are omnivores (not carnivores, as commonly believed), so all balanced dog foods contain animal as well as plant ingredients.

STAGES OF LIFE

When selecting your dog's diet, three stages of development must be considered: the puppy stage, the adult stage, and the senior stage.

Puppy Diets: Pups instinctively want to nurse, and a normal puppy will exhibit this behavior from just a few moments following birth. Puppies should be allowed to nurse for about the first six weeks, although from the third or fourth week, the breeder will begin to introduce small portions of suitable solid food. Most breeders like to introduce alternate milk and meat meals initially, building up to weaning time.

Feeding your dog in his crate is a great way to instill the fact that it is his "den."

How can you tell if your Bulldog is fit or fat?
When you run your hands down your pal's sides from front to back, you should be able to easily feel his ribs. It's OK if you feel a little body fat (and, of course, hair), but you should not feel huge fat pads. You should also be able to feel your Bully's waist— an indentation behind the ribs.

By the time puppies are seven to eight weeks old, they should be fully weaned and fed solely on a proprietary puppy food. Selection of the most suitable, good-quality diet at this time is essential, for a puppy's fastest growth rate is during the first year of life. Seek advice about your dog's food from your veterinarian. The frequency of meals will be reduced over time, and when a young dog has reached the age of ten to twelve months, he should be switched to an adult diet.

Puppy and junior diets should be well balanced for the needs of your Bulldog so that, except in certain circumstances, additional vitamins, minerals, and proteins will not be required.

How many times a day does your Bulldog need to eat? Puppies have small stomachs and high metabolic rates, so they need to eat several times a day in order to consume sufficient nutrients. If your puppy is younger than three months old, feed him four or five meals a day. When your little buddy is three to five months old, decrease the number of meals to three or four. At six months of age, most puppies can move to an adult schedule of two meals a day.

Adult Diets: A dog is considered an adult when he has stopped growing, so in general, the diet of a Bulldog can be changed to an adult one at about nine to twelve months of age. Again, rely on your veterinarian or dietary specialist to recommend an acceptable maintenance diet.

Along with a balanced diet, your Bulldog needs plenty of fresh, clean water.

Major dog food manufacturers specialize in this type of food, and smart owners must select the one best suited to his dog's needs. Do not leave food out all day for "free-choice" feeding, as this freedom inevitably translates to inches around the dog's waist.

Senior Diets: As dogs get older, their metabolisms change. The older dog usually exercises less, moves more slowly, and sleeps more. This change in lifestyle and physiological performance requires a change in diet. Because these changes take place slowly, they might not be recognizable. These metabolic changes increase the tendency toward obesity, requiring an even more vigilant approach to feeding. Obesity in an older Bulldog compounds the health problems that already accompany old age.

As your Bulldog gets older, few of his organs function up to par. The kidneys slow down, and the intestines become less efficient. These age-related factors are best handled with a change in diet and a change in feeding schedule to give smaller portions that are more easily digested.

There isn't a best diet for every older dog. While many dogs do well on light or senior diets, some do better on a special premium diet such as lamb and rice. Be sensitive to your senior Bulldog's diet, and this will help control other problems that may arise with your old Bully friend.

FLATULENCE AND THE BULLDOG

Gas is a normal by-product of your Bulldog's digestion, but too much of it can cause flatu-

lence, as well as abdominal pain and borborygmus (those "rumbly-tummy" noises). It can also make your pal a bit of a social outcast, at least around people.

The most common cause of flatulence is plain old air that a dog swallows while gulping food—an eating style shared by many Bulldogs. Diet can play a role as well: High fiber or high soy diets, spoiled food, and simply overeating can all lead to increased odiferous emissions. Food sensitivities, digestive disorders, intestinal parasites, and gastrointestinal diseases can also cause it.

If your Bulldog suffers from flatulence, you'll need to check with her veterinarian, who can examine your dog and perform tests to determine the cause. The treatment your vet then prescribes will depend on what's causing the problem. If your Bully's flatulence isn't caused by gastrointestinal disease or parasites, the following measures might provide some relief:

Reduce gulping. Feed your dog smaller, more frequent meals or feed him small amounts in different locations throughout the house. If you have more than one dog, feed them separately to decrease competition for food.

Change food. A highly digestible, low-fiber diet may reduce flatulence. If your Bully appears to be sensitive to a particular ingredient, switch to a food that doesn't include it.

Don't allow access to spoiled food. Most dogs will eat rotten food without a second thought. That means you need to monitor what your Bulldog puts in his mouth.

Take a hike, and take your Bulldog with you. Light exercise after eating can reduce gas accumulation.

Medical help: Certain digestive aids such as Acidophilus (helpful bacteria found in the normal digestive tract) and digestive enzyme preparations may lessen gas production by helping your Bulldog digest his food more completely. Simethicone tablets (available without prescription) may also help a gassy Bully.

Note: Be on the side of caution and consult your veterinarian before you give your Bulldog buddy any of the compounds mentioned here.

These delicious, dog-friendly recipes will have your furry friend smacking his lips and salivating for more. Just remember: Treats aren't meant to replace your dog's regular meals. Give your dog snacks sparingly and continue to feed him nutritious, well-balanced meals.

Cheddar Squares

$1/3$ cup all-natural applesauce
$1/3$ cup low-fat cheddar cheese, shredded
$1/3$ cup water
2 cups unbleached white flour

In a medium bowl, mix all wet ingredients. In a large bowl, mix all dry ingredients. Slowly add the wet ingredients to the dry mixture. Mix well. Pour batter into a greased 13x9x2-inch pan. Bake at 375-degrees Fahrenheit for 25 to 30 minutes. Bars are done when a toothpick inserted in the center and removed comes out clean. Cool and cut into bars. Makes about 54 one-and-a-half-inch bars.

Peanut Butter Bites

3 tablespoons vegetable oil
$1/4$ cup smooth peanut butter, no salt or sugar
$1/4$ cup honey
$1 1/2$ teaspoon baking powder
2 eggs
2 cups whole wheat flower

In a large bowl, mix all ingredients until dough is firm. If the dough is too sticky, mix in a small amount of flour. Knead dough on a lightly floured surface until firm. Roll out dough half an inch thick and cut with cookie cutters. Put cookies on a cookie sheet half an inch apart. Bake at 350-degrees Fahrenheit for 20 to 25 minutes. When done, cookies should be firm to the touch. Turn oven off and leave cookies for one to two hours to harden. Makes about 40 two-inch-long cookies.

BULLDOG

A vital factor to glowingly healthy Bulldog skin is regular brushing and bathing. Brushing circulates the skin's natural oils throughout the coat, making it shinier, and helps remove dead hair, encouraging it to regrow. It also gives smart owners the opportunity to check for irritations, rashes, bites, or parasites. This breed's sensitive skin tends to overreact to harsh grooming products and other irritants.

WRINKLES IN TIME

Left untended, a Bulldog's wrinkles and folds become moist and dirty, the perfect environment for inflammation, itching, and infections of all kinds, including bacterial, fungal and yeast infections. For minor irritations or infections, the Bulldog Club of America recommends applying Panalog® ointment, an all-purpose ointment (antifungal, antibacterial, antiyeast and anti-inflammatory); or Bag Balm®, an antiseptic salve with petroleum and lanolin.

Wrinkles that are extremely itchy or harbor a dark or smelly growth require prompt veterinary attention. Without treat-

Did You Know? **Nail clipping can be tricky, so many dog owners leave the task for the professionals.** However, if you walk you dog on concrete, you may not have to worry about it. The concrete acts like a nail file and will probably keep the nails in check.

Bathtime
can be
funtime if
you include
the whole
family!

ment, the problem typically worsens. Once infected, a Bulldog is more likely to suffer the same infection again, and chronic problems may require surgery to fix.

Clean your Bulldog's face, facial wrinkles, and body wrinkles daily, although some do fine with three times a week. The frequency depends on your dog's age, health, and the depth of the wrinkles. The deeper the wrinkles, the greater the likelihood of him developing a problem. And as Bulldogs age, the wrinkles get deeper, making it more difficult to keep them fresh and healthy.

Clean your Bulldog's wrinkles and folds gently using a wash cloth moistened with water or lathered with your dog's shampoo or a mild soap (rinse with clean water afterward). You also can use an unscented, moist towelette; ones containing aloe vera or lanolin are ideal.

Areas to concentrate on include the deep nose wrinkle (also called a roll or pocket) just over the muzzle, the other facial wrinkles, and the tail pocket.

Completely dry the wrinkles afterward with a soft cloth. Some folks even dust talcum powder or cornstarch in the clean folds to keep them drier. Be careful, though, not to get any powder in the dog's eyes.

Give your Bulldog's face a good cleaning after he eats or sticks his face into anything messy, which happens more often than you'd think. Food bits can collect in the facial folds and are far too inviting to unhealthy visitors.

WHILE YOU'RE AT IT

During your daily face cleaning is the optimal time to clean up a few other potential problem areas, too. First, clean the fur around the eyes, then clean any eye goobers, checking the eyes for any scratches or irritation. Dirt and moisture left under the eyes can stain the fur.

Next, wash and dry your dog's nose, removing any mucus or dirt. If cracked skin is a problem, experts suggest placing petroleum jelly on the nose leather (not in the wrinkles) to soothe it. The nose can be kept nice and black by dabbing a bit of baby oil or vitamin E oil on it. Just don't use so much of it that you smother your dog.

Also, check the tail pocket, if your dog has one. This deep fold of skin, which sits above the tail, is highly susceptible to problems. Clean and dry it with the same care you'd use for the nose wrinkle. For a tight pocket, use a cotton ball, rather than a cloth.

Finally, clean your dog's tail. Bulldog tails come in many shapes and sizes. Tightly twisted or kinked tails may develop rashes and infections at the bent parts. Clean and dry the entire tail, including the underside, regularly.

If the tail is corkscrew, follow the tail all the way around with a wash cloth. An inverted tail (a tail that tucks up inside a skin pocket) and tails that are pressed tight against the anus need extra-special care to stay clean.

BRUSHING AND BATHING BASICS

Regular grooming sessions are a good way to spend time with your dog. Many dogs grow to like the feel of being brushed and will enjoy the daily routine.

A natural bristle brush or a hound glove can be used for regular routine brushing. Daily brushing is effective for removing dead hair and stimulating the dog's natural oils to add shine and a healthy look to the coat. Although the Bulldog's coat is short and close, it does require a daily five-minute once-over to keep it looking its shiny best.

Brush your Bulldog thoroughly before giving him a bath. This will get rid of most loose hair, which is harder to remove when the coat is wet. Dogs do not need to be bathed as often as humans, but regular bathing is essential for healthy skin and a clean, shiny coat. If you accustom your dog to being bathed as a puppy, it will be second nature by the time he grows up. You want your dog to be at ease in the bath or else it could end up a wet, soapy, messy ordeal for both of you!

Make sure that your Bulldog has a good non-slip surface to stand on. Begin by wetting the dog's coat. A shower or hose attachment is necessary for thoroughly wetting and rinsing the coat. Check the water temperature to make sure that it is neither too hot nor too cold.

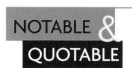
NOTABLE & QUOTABLE

After removing a tick, clean the dog's skin with hydrogen peroxide. If Lyme disease is common where you live, have your veterinarian test the tick. Tick preventive medication will discourage ticks from attaching and kill any that do.

—*groomer Andrea Vilardi from West Paterson, N.J.*

Next, apply shampoo to the dog's coat and work it into a good lather. You should purchase a shampoo that is made for dogs. Do not use a product made for human hair. Wash the head last; you do not want shampoo to drip into the dog's eyes while you are washing the rest of his body. Work the shampoo all the way down to the skin. You can use this opportunity to check the skin for any bumps, bites, or other abnormalities. Do not neglect any area of the body—get all of the hard-to-reach places.

Once your dog has been thoroughly shampooed, he requires an equally thorough rinsing. Shampoo left in the coat can irritate the skin. Protect his eyes from the shampoo by shielding them with your hand and directing the flow of water in the opposite direction. You should also avoid getting water in the ear canal. Be prepared for your dog to shake out his coat—you might want to stand back, but make sure you hold onto the dog to keep him from running through the house.

EAR CLEANING

Your dog's ears should be kept clean and any excess hair inside should be removed. Ears can be cleaned with a cotton ball and special cleaner or ear powder made for dogs. Be on the lookout for any signs of infection or ear-mite infestation. If your Bulldog has been shaking his head or scratching at his ears frequently, this usually indicates a problem. If his ears have an unusual odor, this is a sure sign of mite infestation or infection, and a signal to have his ears checked by the veterinarian.

NAIL CLIPPING

Your Bulldog should be accustomed to having his nails trimmed at an early age because it will be part of your maintenance routine throughout his life. Not only does it look nicer, but long nails can scratch someone unintentionally. Also, a long nail has a better chance of ripping and bleeding, or causing the feet to spread. A good rule of thumb is that if you can hear your dog's nails clicking on the floor when he walks, his nails are too long.

Before you start cutting, make sure you can identify the "quick" in each nail. The quick is a blood vessel that runs through the center of each nail and grows rather close to the end. It will bleed if accidentally cut, which will be quite painful for the dog as it contains nerve endings. Keep some type of clotting agent on hand, such as a styptic pencil or styptic powder (the type used for shaving). This will stop the bleeding quickly when applied to the end of the cut nail. Do not panic if you cut the quick, just stop the bleeding and talk soothingly to your dog. Once he has

NOTABLE & QUOTABLE

Bathe as needed. If your Bulldog gets into the mud, he definitely will need a bath. However, once every four to six weeks is usually enough for a healthy dog.

—Darlene Stuedemann of Clinton, Iowa, a breeder and an exhibitor

Praise and treats go a long way when teaching your Bully to enjoy bathtime.

Bulldogs don't need to be bathed often, unless they get dirty while playing in the lake or splashing in a mud puddle!

calmed down, move on to the next nail. It is better to clip a little at a time, particularly with black-nailed dogs.

Hold your pup steady as you begin trimming his nails; you do not want him to make any sudden movements or run away. Talk to him in a calm tone and stroke him as you clip. Holding his foot in your hand, simply take off the end of each nail in one quick clip. You can purchase nail clippers that are specially made for dogs; you can find them wherever you buy pet supplies.

TIPTOP TOES

Apply petroleum jelly if your Bulldog gets dry, cracked foot pads.

Trim the hair between the toes and on the feet weekly so your dog isn't as likely to pick up debris. Check for and remove any objects while you're at it.

Also look between the toes for interdigital cysts, which are small, red swellings that make it painful for the dog to walk, particularly on the forepaws. These may be caused by debris, such as burrs, seeds, or small rocks,

JOIN OUR ONLINE Bulldog Club

Every Bulldog should look beautiful. What do you need to keep your pup looking his best? Go to Club Bulldog (**DogChannel.com/ Club-Bulldog**) and download a checklist of essential grooming equipment you and your Bully will need.

that get caught in the fur between the toes and pushed up into the foot pads.

If your dog does develop a cyst, remove whatever might be causing it. Clean the area, then soak the paw in a mixture of warm water and Epsom salts for two to four minutes. Dry, and rub in anti-inflammatory ointment. Take him to the veterinarian if the cyst doesn't improve.

DENTAL DUTIES

Like many people, Bulldogs can suffer from dental disease, so veterinary experts recommend brushing your dog's teeth on a regular basis. Daily brushing is best, but your dog will benefit from tooth brushing a few times a week. The teeth should be

SMART TIP!

Ideally, brush your Bulldog's coat three times a week. Start at the rear end, brushing against the grain, then brush with the grain, to get the most dead hair out and stimulate the skin. If you'd like, burnish the coat with a soft cloth to add more shine.

white and free of yellowish tartar, and the gums should appear healthy and pink. Gums that bleed easily when you perform dental duties may have gingivitis.

The first thing to know is that your puppy probably isn't going to want your fingers in his mouth. Desensitizing your puppy—getting him to accept that you will be looking at

and touching his teeth—is the first step to overcoming his reticence. You can begin this as soon as you get your puppy, with the help of the thing that motivates him most: food.

For starters, let your puppy lick some chicken, vegetable, or beef broth off your finger. Then, dip your finger in broth again, and gently insert your finger in the side of your dog's mouth. Touch his side teeth and gums. Several sessions will get your puppy used to having his mouth touched.

Use a toothbrush specifically made for a dog or a finger-tip brush wrapped around your finger to brush your Bulldog's teeth. Hold the mouth with the fingers of one hand, and brush with the other. Use toothpaste made for dogs with dog-slurping flavors like poultry and beef. The human kind froths too much and can give your dog an upset stomach if swallowed. Brush in a circular motion with the brush held at a forty-five-degree angle to the gum line. Be sure to get the fronts, tops, and sides of each tooth.

Look for signs of plaque, tartar, or gum disease, including redness, swelling, foul breath, discolored enamel near the gum line and receding gums. If you see these, take your Bulldog to the veterinarian immediately. Also see your vet about once a year for a dental checkup.

BEHIND THE BULLDOG

Your Bulldog's tail needs special care, too. Is your dog scooting his butt, biting or licking at his perineum (the area between the anus and the genitals) or hind legs, or chasing his tail? These may be signs that his anal glands (or anal sacs) need attention.

Located on either side of a dog's anus, the anal glands gradually secrete a thick, smelly fluid as the dog walks or defecates. When a gland's duct becomes blocked, the fluid can build up and cause irritation and itching, which is why the scooting happens. If the gland becomes infected, it may abscess and burst, causing no end of health trouble.

A blockage might occur due to bacterial infection, injuries, or tapeworm infestation. Obesity, lack of muscle tone, lack of exercise, and chronic diarrhea may also contribute.

Once you notice a problem, your veterinarian can manually express the glands, but it may take several trips to completely empty them. If the scooting doesn't stop in a few days, consult with your veterinarian because something else may be wrong. For chronic anal gland concerns, you may need to have your dog's glands expressed every two to six months.

REMOVING TEAR STAINS

Many Bulldogs, especially light-colored ones, develop tear stains. Dirt and moisture collect below the eyes, which is the ideal place for a bacterial or yeast infection, leading to ugly, reddish-brown stains. These may be due to your Bulldog's diet, excessive tearing, infections, or parasites. Clear up these issues first, or the tear stains will continue to be an issue.

To minimize staining, clean the fur under the eyes with a wet wash cloth or moist towelette when you clean your Bulldog's facial wrinkles.

Many commercial stain removers are available. Try a variety to see which one works best for your dog, and use as directed.

Or try this homemade tear-stain remover,

Did You Know? The crunchiness of unmoistened dry dog food helps keep teeth healthy by reducing plaque accumulation and massaging the gums.

A good grooming routine is not only good for your dog's body, but it keeps him feeling better mentally, as well.

recommended by the Bulldog Club of America. Mix 1 tablespoon hydrogen peroxide with just enough cornstarch to form a paste. Spread this paste on the tear stains, allow it to dry, then brush it off. Use it daily until the stain disappears, then use it weekly to prevent it from coming back. Or clean under your dog's eyes on a daily basis with a cotton ball soaked in boric acid until the stains are gone, then on a weekly basis.

MORE CONCERNS

In addition to irritated and infected wrinkles, your Bulldog may display other skin issues. They could be due to parasites; allergies; fungal, yeast, or bacterial infections; or diseases, such as hypothyroidism. Most skin problems are due to allergies, ranging from moisture from grass clippings, to fertilizer to food allergies to pollen in the air.

Consult your veterinarian if your Bulldog shows any of these symptoms:

Eczema or canine atopic dermatitis: symptoms include itchy, inflamed, dry skin, which often flares up into dry, scaly skin with lumps or blisters, or wet, open sores, especially during hot weather. May be attributed to allergies, insect bites, hormonal imbalances, or stress.

Facial acne: Symptoms are small, pink pimples and blackheads on the face, chin, lips, and muzzle. Facial acne is often due to an allergic reaction but may have other causes. Minor cases may not be itchy or painful. However, in some cases, it may lead to infection, pain, and intense itching.

Fungal spots: Symptoms include red, itchy spots, similar to hot spots, but drier, with scabs or crusts. They're caused by a fungal infection, such as ringworm.

General allergic reaction: Symptoms include itching, scratching, and biting at the skin. Although the cause is difficult to determine, your dog may be reacting to food, airborne irritants, or parasites, such as fleas.

Hot spots: Symptoms of hot spots include red, moist, hairless, extremely itchy round spots. These can worsen quickly as the dog picks at the area, causing additional itching and damage. This is usually caused by allergic reactions but may also

occur after grooming in response to inflammation or a contact allergy.

Insect stings: Symptoms include very small, round, red spots. Cover with an ice pack and monitor the sting area for about thirty minutes. Life-threatening allergic reactions include swelling, hives and difficulty breathing. In this case, take your Bulldog to the vet as quickly as possible.

Seasonal flank alopecia: Symptoms include a loss of coat over the ribs, flanks, and hindquarters that is often symmetrical. The skin may darken, thicken, and develop a polished look or it may flake, scale, and dry out. SFA isn't generally painful or itchy. It begins in mid- to late winter and generally goes away by mid-summer. Because this problem is more common in the wintery, northern areas, one theory states it's triggered by lack of exposure to sunlight.

Seborrhea: Skin and coat become either overly oily and greasy, or extremely dry and dull with dandruff, due to excessive, abnormal discharge from the sebaceous glands of the skin. This usually causes itching and irritation, making the dog scratch, which may lead to a secondary infection. The cause may be unknown or it may come on top of another inflammatory skin problem.

If you can hear your Bully's nails as he walks across the floor (left), it's time to trim his nails (opposite page).

TRAIN

In order for a smart owner to teach his Bulldog anything, he must first get the dog's attention. After all, your dog can't learn anything if he is looking away from you with his mind on something else. Remember that your Bulldog does not understand your verbal language, he only recognizes sounds. Your question translates to a series of sounds for him, and those sounds become the signal to go to you and pay attention; if he does, he will get to interact with you plus receive treats and praise.

Reward-based training methods—clicker and luring—show dogs what to do and help them do it correctly, setting them up for success and rewards rather than mistakes and punishment.

Most dogs find food rewards meaningful. This works well because positive training relies on using treats to encourage the dog to offer a behavior. The treat is then given as a reward. When you reinforce desired behaviors with rewards that are valuable to your Bulldog, you're met with happy cooperation rather than resistance.

Did You Know? The prime period for socialization is short. Most behavior experts agree that positive experiences during the ten-week period between four and fourteen weeks of age are vital to the development of a puppy into an adult dog with sound temperament.

If your Bulldog refuses to sit with both haunches squarely beneath him and instead sits on one side or the other, he may have a physical reason for doing so. Discuss the habit with your veterinarian to be certain that your dog isn't suffering from some structural problem.

Positive does not mean permissive. While you are rewarding your Bulldog's desirable behaviors, you must manage him to be sure he doesn't get rewarded for undesirable behaviors. Training tools, such as leashes, tethers, baby gates, and crates, help keep your dog out of trouble, and the use of force-free negative punishment (the dog's behavior makes a good thing go away) helps him realize that there are negative consequences for inappropriate behaviors.

LEARNING SOCIAL GRACES

Now that you have done all of the preparatory work and have helped your Bulldog get accustomed to his new home and family, it is time for you to have some fun! Socializing your Bulldog puppy gives you the opportunity to show off your new friend, and your pup gets to reap the benefits of being an adorable little creature that people will want to pet and, in general, think is absolutely precious!

Besides getting to know his new family, your pup should be exposed to other people, animals, and situations, but of course he must not come into close contact with dogs you don't know well until he has had all his vaccinations. This will help him become well adjusted as he grows up, and less prone to being timid or fearful of the new things.

Your Bulldog puppy's socialization began at the breeder's home, but now it is your responsibility to continue it. The socialization he receives up until the age of twelve weeks is the most critical, as this is the time when he forms his impressions of the outside world. Be especially careful during the eight- to ten-week period, also known as the fear period. The interaction he receives during this time should be gentle and reassuring. Lack of socialization can manifest itself in fear and aggression as your dog grows up. Your Bulldog puppy needs lots of human contact, affection, handling, and exposure to other animals.

Once your puppy has received his necessary vaccinations, feel free to take him out and about (on his leash, of course). Walk him around the neighborhood, take him on your daily errands, let people pet him, let him

A good temperament is genetic; good manners are learned.

If you want to make your dog happy, create a digging spot where he's allowed to disrupt the earth. Encourage him to dig there by burying bones and toys, and helping him dig them up.

—Pat Miller, a certified pet dog trainer in Hagerstown, Md.

public market is fine; two hours at a loud outdoor concert is too much. Meeting vaccinated, tolerant, and gentle older dogs is great. Meeting dogs you don't know isn't a great idea, especially if they appear very energetic, dominant, or fearful. Control the situations in which you place your Bulldog puppy.

The best way to socialize your puppy to a new experience is to make him think it's the best thing ever. You can do this with a lot of happy talk, enthusiasm, and, yes, food.

To convince your puppy that almost any experience is a blast, always carry treats. Consider carrying two types—a bag of his puppy chow, which you can give him when introducing him to nonthreatening experiences, and a bag of high-value, mouth-watering treats to give him when introducing him to scarier experiences.

BASIC CUES

All Bulldogs, regardless of your training and relationship goals, need to know at least five basic good manners behaviors: sit, down, stay, come, and heel. Here are tips for teaching your dog these important cues.

SIT: Every dog should learn how to sit on command.

▲ Hold a treat at the end of your Bulldog's nose.

▲ Move the treat over his head.

▲ When your Bulldog sits, click a clicker or say "yes!"

▲ Feed your dog the treat.

▲ If your dog jumps up, hold the treat lower. If he backs up, back him into a corner and wait until he sits. Be patient. Keep your clicker handy, and click (or say "yes!") and treat anytime he offers a sit.

▲ When he offers sits easily, say "sit" just before he offers, so he can make the association between the word and the behavior.

meet other dogs and pets. Make sure to expose your Bulldog to different people—men, women, kids, babies, men with beards, teenagers with cell phones or riding skateboards, joggers, shoppers, someone in a wheelchair, a pregnant woman, etc. Make sure your Bulldog explores different surfaces like sidewalks, gravel, a puddle. Positive experience is the key to building confidence. It's up to you to make sure your Bulldog safely discovers the world so he will be a calm, confident, and well-socialized dog.

It's important that you take the lead in all socialization experiences and never put your puppy into a scary or potentially harmful situation. Be mindful of your Bulldog's limitations. Fifteen minutes at a

Add the sit cue when you know you can get the behavior. Your dog doesn't know what the word means until you repeatedly associate it with the appropriate behavior.

▲ When your Bulldog sits easily on cue, start using intermittent reinforcement by clicking some sits but not others. At first, click most sits and skip an occasional one (this is a high rate of reinforcement). Gradually make your clicks more and more random.

DOWN: If your dog can sit, he can lie down, and "down" is one of the easiest cues for Bulldogs because they exist in a nearly prone position.

▼ Have your dog sit.

▼ Hold the treat in front of his nose. Move it down slowly, straight toward the floor (toward his toes). If he follows all the way down, click and treat.

▼ If your Bulldog gets stuck, move the treat down more slowly. Click and treat for small movements downward—moving his head a bit lower, or inching one paw forward. Keep clicking and treating until he is all the way down. This is called shaping—rewarding small pieces of a behavior until your dog succeeds.

▼ If he stands as you move the treat toward the floor, have him sit, and move the treat more slowly downward, shaping with clicks and treats for small movements down as long as he is sitting. If he stands, cheerfully say "Oops!" (which means "Sorry, no treat for that!"), have him sit, and try again.

▼ If shaping isn't working, sit on the floor with your knee raised. Have your Bulldog sit

Using treats during training lessons will go a long way to enticing this food-loving breed.

JOIN OUR ONLINE **Bulldog Club**

With the proper training, your Bulldog will be as well-behaved as he is adorable. One certification that all dogs should receive is the American Kennel Club Canine Good Citizen, which rewards dogs with good manners. Go to **DogChannel.com/Club-Bulldog** and click on "downloads" to get the ten steps required for your dog to be a CGC.

next to you. Put your hand with the treat under your knee and lure him under your leg so that he lies down and crawls to follow the treat. Click and treat!

▼ When you can lure the down easily, add the verbal cue, wait a few seconds to let your dog think, then lure him down to show him the association. Repeat until he'll go down on the verbal cue. Then begin using intermittent reinforcement.

STAY: What good are the sit and down cues if your dog doesn't stay?

■ Start with your Bulldog in the sit or down position.

■ Put the treat in front of his nose and keep it there.

■ Click and reward several times while he is in position, then release him with a cue that you will always use to tell him the stay is over. Common release cues are: "all done," "break," "free," "free dog," "at ease," and "OK."

■ When your dog will stay in a sit or down position while you click and treat, add your verbal stay cue. Say "stay," pause for a second or two, click and say "stay" again. Then, release him from the position.

■ When he's getting the idea, say "stay," whisk the treat out of sight behind your back, click, and whisk the treat back. Be sure to get it all the way to his nose, so he doesn't jump up. Gradually increase the duration of the stay.

■ When your dog will stay for fifteen to twenty seconds, add small distractions: shuffling your feet, moving your arms, small hops. Increase distractions very gradually. If he makes mistakes, you're adding too much too fast.

■ When he'll stay for fifteen to twenty seconds with distractions, gradually add distance. Have your Bulldog stay, take a half-step back, click, return, and treat.

When he'll stay with a half-step, tell him to stay, take a full step back, click, and return. Always return to your dog to treat after you click, but before you release him. If you always return, his stay becomes strong. If you call him to you, his stay gets weaker due to his eagerness to come to you.

Even the best dogs have some bad habits. If you are frustrated with a particular behavior that your Bulldog exhibits, don't despair! Go online and join Club Bulldog, where you can ask other Bully owners for advice on dealing with excessive digging, stubbornness, house-training issues and more. Log on to **DogChannel.com/Club-Bulldog** and click on "community."

JOIN OUR ONLINE **Bulldog Club**

Knowing good-manners cues is a big help, especially when you're out in public with your Bulldog.

COME: Coming when called can be a challenging behavior to teach. It is possible, however. To succeed, you need to install an automatic response to your "come" cue—one so automatic that your dog doesn't even stop to think when he hears it, but will spin on his heels and charge to you at full speed.

Did You Know?

Once your Bulldog understands what behavior goes with a specific cue, it is time to start weaning him off the food treats. At first, give a treat after each exercise. Then, give a treat only after every other exercise. Mix up the times when you offer a food reward and the times when you only offer praise so that your dog will never know when he is going to receive both food and praise and when he is going to receive only praise.

● Start by charging a come cue word the same way you charged your clicker. If your Bulldog already ignores the word "come," pick a different cue, like "front" or "hugs." Say your cue and feed him a bit of scrumptious treat, like boiled chicken. Repeat this until his eyes light up when he hears the cue. Now you're ready to start training.

● With your dog on a leash, run away several steps and cheerfully call out your charged cue. When he follows, click the clicker. Feed him a treat when he reaches you. For a more enthusiastic come, run away at full speed as you call him. When he follows at a gallop, click, stop running, and give him a treat. The better your dog gets at coming, the farther away he can be when you call him.

● Once your Bulldog understands the come cue, play with more people, each with a clicker and treats. Stand a short dis-

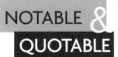

NOTABLE & QUOTABLE

The Bulldog is a very affectionate animal with his own agenda. I find their stubborn natures comical as I watch their minds choose to obey or not, depending on what's in their best interest.

—Bulldog rescue group coordinator Debbie Paxton of Clifton Forge, Va.

tance apart and take turns calling and running away. Click and treat in turn as he comes to each of you. Gradually increase the distance until he comes flying to each person from a distance.

● When you're ready to practice in wide-open spaces, attach a long line—a twenty- to fifty-foot leash—so you can gather him up if that squirrel is too much of a temptation. Then go practice where there are less tempting distractions.

HEEL: Heeling means that your Bulldog walks beside you without pulling. It takes time and patience on your part to succeed at teaching your dog that you will not proceed unless he is walking calmly beside you. Pulling out ahead on the leash is definitely not acceptable.

❍ Begin by holding the leash in your left hand as your dog sits beside your left leg. Move the loop end of the leash to your right hand but keep your left hand short on the leash so that it keeps the dog close to you.

❍ Say "heel" and step forward on your left foot. Keep your dog close to you and take three steps. Stop and have your dog sit next to you in what we now call the heel position. Praise verbally, but do not touch the dog. Hesitate a moment and begin

again with "heel," taking three steps and stopping. Then, tell your dog to sit.

❍ Your goal here is to have your Bulldog walk those three steps without pulling on the leash. Once he will walk calmly beside you for three steps without pulling, increase the number of steps you take to five. When he will walk politely beside you while you take five steps, you can increase the length of your walk to ten steps. Keep increasing the length of your stroll until your dog will walk quietly beside you without pulling as long as you want him to heel. When you stop heeling, indicate to your dog that the exercise is over by verbally praising as you pet him and say "OK, good dog." The "OK" is used as a release word, meaning that the exercise is finished, and the dog is free to relax.

❍ If you are dealing with a dog who insists on pulling you around, simply "put on your brakes" and stand your ground until he realizes that the two of you are not going anywhere until he is beside you and moving at your pace, not his. It may take some time just standing there to convince your dog that you are the leader, and you will be the one to decide on the direction and speed of your travel.

❍ Each time your Bulldog looks up at you or slows down to give a slack leash between the two of you, quietly praise him and say, "Good heel. Good dog." Eventually, your dog will begin to respond, and within a few days, he will be walking politely beside you without pulling on the leash. At first, the training sessions should be kept short and positive; soon, your dog will be able to walk nicely with you for increasingly longer distances. Remember to give him free time and the opportunity to run and play when you have finished heel practice.

TRAINING TIPS

If not properly socialized, managed, and trained, even well-bred Bulldogs will offer raw material for undesirable behaviors such as jumping up, barking, chasing, chewing, and other destructive behaviors. You can prevent these annoying habits and help your Bulldog become the perfect dog you're hoping for by following some basic training and behavior tenets.

1. Be consistent. Consistency is important, not just in relation to what you allow your dog to do (get on the sofa, perhaps) and not do (jump up on people) but also in the verbal and body language cues you use with your dog and in his daily routine.

2. Be gentle but firm. Positive training methods are becoming the norm. Dog-friendly methods, properly applied, are wonderfully effective, creating canine-

SMART TIP!

It's a good idea to enroll in an obedience class if one is available in your area. Many cities have dog clubs that offer basic obedience training as well as preparatory classes for obedience competition. Local dog trainers may offer similar classes.

human relationships based on mutual respect and cooperation.

3. Manage behavior. All living things repeat behaviors that reward them. Behaviors that aren't reinforced will go away.

4. Provide adequate exercise. A tired dog is a well-behaved dog. Many behavior problems can be avoided, others resolved, simply by providing your Bulldog with enough exercise.

THE THREE-STEP PROGRAM

Perhaps it's too late to give your Bulldog consistency, training, and management from the start. Maybe he came from a Bull-

Everyone in the family should get into the habit of training your Bulldog, including the kids.

dog rescue or a shelter, or you didn't realize the importance of these tenets when he was a pup. He already may have learned some undesirable behaviors. Perhaps they're even part of your Bulldog genetic package. Many unwanted behaviors can be modified with relative ease using the following three-step process for changing an unwanted behavior.

Step No. 1: Visualize the behavior you want. If you simply try to stop your dog from doing something, you leave a behavior vacuum. You need to fill that vacuum with something, so your dog doesn't return to the same behavior or fill it with one that's even worse! If you're tired of your Bulldog jumping up, decide what you'd prefer instead. A Bulldog who greets people by sitting politely in front of them is a joy to own.

Step No. 2: Prevent your Bulldog from being rewarded for the behavior you don't want. Management to the rescue! When your Bulldog jumps up to greet you or get your attention, turn your back and step away to show him that jumping up no longer works to gain attention. Step through a door, if necessary.

Step No. 3: Generously reinforce the desired behavior. Remember, dogs repeat behaviors that reward them. If your Bulldog no longer gets attention for jumping up and is heavily reinforced with attention and treats for sitting, he will offer sits instead of jumping, because sits get him what he wants.

COUNTER CONDITIONING

Behaviors that respond well to the three-step process are those where the dog does something in order to get good stuff. He jumps up to get attention. He nips at your hands to get you to play with him.

Counter conditioning is an easy and fun way to socialize your Bulldog to unfamiliar people and places.

The three steps don't work well when you're dealing with behaviors that are based in strong emotion, such as aggression and fear, or with hardwired behaviors such as chasing prey. With these, you can change the emotional or hardwired response through counter conditioning—programming a new emotional or automatic response to the stimulus by giving it a new association.

Here's how you would counter condition a Bulldog who chases after skateboarders—maybe he wants to ride, too—when you're walking him on a leash.

■ Have a large supply of very high-value treats, such as canned chicken.

■ Station yourself with your Bulldog on a leash at a location where skateboarders will pass by at a subthreshold distance "X"—that is, where your Bulldog alerts but doesn't lunge and bark.

■ Wait for a skateboarder. The instant your Bulldog notices the skateboarder, feed him bits of chicken, nonstop, until the skateboard is gone. Stop feeding him the chicken.

■ Repeat many times until, when the skateboarder appears, your Bulldog looks at you with a big grin as if to say, "Yay! Where's my chicken?" This is a conditioned emotional response, or CER.

■ When you have a consistent CER at X, decrease the distance slightly, perhaps minus one foot, and repeat until you consistently get the CER at this distance.

■ Keep decreasing the distance and obtain a CER at each level, until a skateboarder goes right past, eliciting the "Where's my chicken?" CER. Now return to distance X and add a second skateboarder. Continue this desensitization until your dog doesn't respond to a group of skateboarders.

BAD HABITS

Discipline—training people to act in accordance with rules—brings order to life. It's as simple as that. Without discipline, particularly in a group society, chaos reigns supreme, and the group eventually will perish. Humans and canines are social animals and need some form of discipline in order to function effectively. Dogs need discipline in their lives to understand how their pack (you and other family members) functions and how they must act in order to survive.

Luckily, puppies are little sponges, waiting to soak up whatever information they can, be it bad habits or good manners. Start training early, and you can control what behaviors go into your Bully.

Living with an untrained dog is a lot like owning a piano that you do not know how to play—it's nice to look at, but it doesn't do much more than that to bring you pleasure. Now try taking piano lessons, and suddenly the piano comes alive and brings forth magical sounds and rhythms that set your heart singing and your body swaying.

Did You Know?

Anxiety can make a dog really miserable. Living in a world with scary monsters and suspected Bulldog-eaters roaming the streets must be nerve-wracking. The good news is that timid dogs are not doomed to forever be ruled by fear. Smart owners who understand the timid Bulldog's needs can help him build self-confidence and a more optimistic view of life.

The golden rule of dog training is simple. For each "question" (cue), there is only one correct answer (reaction). One command equals one reaction. Keep practicing the command until the dog reacts correctly without hesitation. Be repetitive but not monotonous. Dogs get bored just as people do; a bored dog's attention will not be focused on the lesson.

The same is true with your Bulldog. Any dog is a big responsibility, and if not trained, may develop unacceptable behavior that annoys you or could even cause family friction.

To train a Bulldog, smart owners should consider enrolling in an obedience class. Your dog learns good manners while you learn how and why he behaves the way he does. Find out how to communicate with your dog and how to recognize and understand his communications with you. Suddenly, your dog takes on a new role in your life—he is smart, interesting, well-behaved, and fun to be with. He demonstrates his bond of devotion to you daily. In other words, your Bulldog does wonders for your ego because he constantly reminds you that you are not only his leader, you are also his hero!

Training dogs when they are puppies results in the highest rate of success in developing well-mannered and well-adjusted adult dogs. Training an older dog, from six months to six years of age, can produce almost equal results, provided that the owner accepts the dog's slower rate of learning capability and is willing to work patiently to help the dog succeed. Unfortunately, many owners of untrained adult dogs lack the patience factor, so they do not persist until their dogs really are successful at learning particular behaviors.

Training a puppy aged ten to sixteen weeks (twenty weeks at the most) is like working with a dry sponge in a pool of water. The pup soaks up whatever you show him and constantly looks for more things to do and learn. At this early age, his body is not yet producing hormones, and therein lies the reason for such a high rate of success. Without hormones, he is focused on his owners and not particularly interested in investigating other places, dogs, people, etc.

You are his leader—his provider of food, water, shelter and security. He latches on to you and wants to stay close. Your dog usually will follow you from room to room, will not let you out of his sight when you are outdoors with him, and will respond in like manner to the people and animals you encounter. If you greet a friend warmly, he will be happy to greet the person as well. If, however, you are hesitant, even anxious, about the approach of a stranger, he will respond accordingly.

Are you causing unnecessary temptation by leaving your footwear in easy-to-reach places? Bad behavior usually traces its roots back to the owner!

Once your puppy begins to produce hormones, his natural curiosity emerges, and he begins to investigate the world around him. It is at this time that you may notice that the untrained dog will begin to wander away from you and will even ignore your commands to stay close.

There are usually dog training classes near you, but you can do a lot to train your dog yourself. This chapter is devoted to helping you train your Bulldog at home. If the recommended procedures are followed faithfully, you can expect positive results.

Whether your new charge is a puppy or a mature adult, the methods of teaching and the techniques used in training basic behaviors are the same. After all, no dog, whether puppy or adult, likes harsh or inhumane methods. All creatures, however, respond favorably to gentle motivational methods, sincere praise, and lots of encouragement.

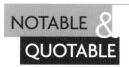

NOTABLE & QUOTABLE

Bulldogs are extremely trainable. In fact, there are several Bulldogs in agility events and with performance titles in obedience and rally. The number of Bulldogs in the performance community is increasing. —Christine Aaron, a breeder in Reston, Va.

The following behavioral problems are the ones which owners most commonly encounter. Every dog is unique and every situation is unique. Because behavioral abnormalities are the leading reason for owners' abandoning their pets, we hope that you will make a valiant effort to solve your Bulldog's problems.

NIP NIPPING

As puppies start to teethe, they feel the need to sink their teeth into anything—unfortunately that includes your fingers, arms, hair, toes, whatever happens to be available. You may find this behavior cute for about the first five seconds—until you feel just how sharp those puppy teeth are. This is something you want to discourage immediately and consistently with a firm "No!" (or whatever number of firm "No"s it takes for your dog to understand that you mean business), and replace your finger with an appropriate chew toy.

STOP THAT WHINING

A puppy will often cry, whine, whimper, howl, or make some type of commotion when he is left alone. This is basically his way of calling out for attention, of calling out

to make sure that you know he is there and that you have not forgotten about him. He feels insecure when he is left alone; for example, when you are out of the house and he is in his crate, or when you are in another part of the house and he cannot see you. The noise he is making is an expression of the anxiety he feels at being left alone, so he needs to be taught that being alone is OK. You are not actually training your dog to stop making noise, you are training him to feel comfortable when he is alone and thus removing the need to make the noise.

This is where the crate with a cozy blanket and a toy comes in handy. You want to know that your pup is safe when you are not there to supervise, and you know that he will be safe in his crate, rather than roaming freely about the house. In order for your Bulldog pup to stay in his crate without making a fuss, he needs to be comfortable in his crate. Also, it is extremely important that the crate is never used as a form of punishment, or your pup will have a negative association with the crate.

Your Bulldog may howl, whine, or otherwise vocalize his displeasure at your leaving the house and his being left alone. This is a normal case of separation anxiety, but there are things that can be done to eliminate this problem. Your dog needs to learn that he will be fine on his own for a while and that he will not wither away if he is not attended to every minute of the day.

In fact, constant attention can lead to separation anxiety in the first place. If you are endlessly coddling and cuddling your Bulldog, he will come to expect this from you all of the time, and it will be more traumatic for him when you are not there.

Obviously, you enjoy spending time with your dog, and he thrives on your love and attention. However, it should not become a dependent relationship where he is heartbroken without you.

One thing you can do to minimize separation anxiety is to make your entrances and exits as low-key as possible. Do not give your dog a long, drawn-out goodbye, and do not lavish him with hugs and kisses when you return. This is giving in to the attention that he craves, and it will only make him miss it more when you are away. Another thing you can try is to give your dog a treat when you leave; this not only will keep him occupied and keep his mind off the fact that you just left, but it also will help him associate your leaving with a pleasant experience.

You may have to accustom your dog to being left alone in intervals, much like when you introduced your pup to his crate. Of course, when your Bulldog starts whimpering as you approach the door, your first instinct will be to run to him and comfort him, but don't do it! Eventually he will adjust and be just fine if you take it in small steps. His anxiety stems from being placed in an unfamiliar situation; by familiarizing him with being alone he will learn that he is okay. That is not to say you should purposely leave your dog home alone, but your dog needs to know that while he can depend on you for his care, you do not have to be by his side twenty-four hours a day.

When your dog is alone in the house, he should be confined to his crate or a designated dog-proof area of the house. This should be the area in which he sleeps, so he should already feel comfortable there and this should make him feel more at ease when he is alone. This is just one of the many examples in which a crate is an invaluable tool for you and your dog, and another reinforcement of why your dog should view his crate as a happy place, and a place of his own.

Accustom your puppy to the crate in short, gradually increasing intervals of time, maybe with a treat, and stay in the room with him. If he cries or makes a fuss, do not go to him, but stay in his sight. Gradually, he will realize that staying in his crate is all right, and it will not be so traumatic for him when you are not around. You may want to leave the radio on softly when you leave the house; the sound of human voices can be comforting to him.

CHEW ON THIS

The national canine pastime is chewing! Every dog loves to sink his "canines" into a tasty bone, but most anything will do! Dogs need to chew to massage their gums, to make their new teeth feel better and to exercise their jaws. This is a natural behavior deeply imbedded in all things canine.

Our role as smart owners is not to stop the chewing, but to redirect it to positive, chew-worthy objects. Be an informed owner and purchase proper chew toys for your Bulldog, like strong nylon bones made for large dogs. Be sure that the toys you choose are safe and durable, because your dog's safety is at risk.

The best answer is prevention: That is, put your shoes, handbags, and other tasty objects in their proper places (out of the reach of the growing canine mouth). Direct your puppy to his toys whenever you see him tasting the furniture legs or the leg of your pants. Make a loud noise to attract your Bulldog pup's attention, and immediately escort him to his chew toy. Engage him with the toy for at least four minutes, praising and encouraging him all the while.

NO MORE JUMPING

Jumping up is a dog's friendly way of saying hello! Some dog owners do not mind when their dogs jump up, which is fine for them. The problem arises when guests come to the house, and the dog greets them in the same manner—whether they like it or not! However friendly the greeting may be, chances are that your visitors will not appreciate your dog's enthusiasm. The dog will not be able to distinguish upon whom he can jump and whom he cannot. Therefore, it is best to discourage this behavior entirely.

Stage false departures. Pick up your car keys and put on your coat, then put them away and go about your routine. Do this several times a day, ignoring your dog while you do it. Soon his reaction to these triggers will decrease.

—September Morn, a dog trainer and behavior specialist in Bellingham, Wash.

Pick a command such as "Off" (avoid using "Down" because you will use that for the dog to lie down) and tell him "Off" when he jumps up. Place him on the ground on all fours and have him sit, praising him the whole time. Always lavish him with praise and petting when he is in the sit position. That way you are still giving him a warm affectionate greeting, because you are as pleased to see him as he is to see you!

UNWANTED BARKING MUST GO

Barking is a dog's way of talking. It can be somewhat frustrating because it is not easy to tell what a dog means by his bark: is he excited, happy, frightened, angry? Whatever it is the dog is trying to say, he should not be punished for barking. It is only when the barking becomes excessive, and when the excessive barking becomes a bad habit, that the behavior needs to be modified.

Chewing isn't a problem. It's what he chews that may be the problem. Make sure your Bully has plenty of chew toys to fulfill his chew desires.

SMART TIP!

Do not carry your puppy to his relief area. Lead him there on a leash or, better yet, encourage him to follow you to the spot. If you start carrying him, you might end up doing this routine for months, and your dog will have the satisfaction of having trained you.

If an intruder came into your home in the middle of the night and your dog barked a warning, wouldn't you be pleased? You would probably deem your dog a hero, a wonderful guardian and protector of the home. On the other hand, if a friend drops by unexpectedly and rings the doorbell and is greeted with a sudden sharp bark, you probably would be annoyed at your dog. But isn't it just the same behavior? The dog does not know any better...unless he sees who is at the door and it is someone he is familiar with, he will bark as a means of vocalizing that his (and your) territory is being threatened. While your friend is not posing a threat, it is all the same to the dog. Barking is his means of letting you know that there is an intrusion, whether friend or foe, on your property. This type of barking is instinctive and should not be discouraged.

Excessive habitual barking, however, is a problem that should be corrected early on. As your Bulldog grows up, you will be able to tell when his barking is purposeful and when it is for no reason. You will become able to distinguish your dog's different barks and with what they are associated. For example, the bark when someone comes to the door will be different from the bark when he is excited to see you. It is similar to a person's tone of voice, except that the dog has to rely totally on tone of voice because he does not have the benefit of using words. An incessant barker will be evident at an early age.

There are some things that encourage a dog to bark. For example, if your dog barks nonstop for a few minutes and you give him a treat to quiet him, he believes that you are rewarding him for barking. He will associate barking with getting a treat, and will keep doing it until he is rewarded.

STOP FOOD STEALING AND BEGGING

Is your dog devising ways of stealing food from your cupboards? If so, you must answer the following questions: Is your Bulldog really hungry? Why is there food on the coffee table? Face it, some dogs are more food-motivated than others; some dogs are totally obsessed by a slab of brisket and can only think of their next meal. Food stealing is terrific fun and always yields a great reward—food, glorious food!

The owner's goal, therefore, is to make the "reward" less rewarding, even startling! Plant a shaker can (an empty can with coins inside) on the table so that when you shake it, your pooch is caught off-guard. There are other devices available that will surprise the dog when he is looking for a mid-afternoon snack. Such remote-control devices, though not the first choice of some trainers, allow the correction to come from the object instead of the owner. These devices are also useful to keep the snacking hound from napping on furniture that is forbidden.

Just like food stealing, begging is a favorite pastime of hungry puppies with that same reward—food! Dogs quickly learn that humans love that feed-me pose and that their selfish owners keep the "good food" for themselves. Why would humans dine on kibble alone when they can cook up sausages and kielbasa? Begging is a conditioned response related to a specific stimulus, time, and place. The sounds of the kitchen, cans and bottles opening, crinkling bags, and the smell of food in preparation will excite the chowhound and soon the paws are in the air!

Here is the solution to stopping this behavior: Never give in to a beggar, no matter how cute or desperate he looks! Do not reward your dog for jumping up, whining, and rubbing his nose into you by giving him that glorious reward—food. By ignoring the dog, you will (eventually) force the behavior into extinction. Note that the behavior likely gets worse before it disappears, so be sure there aren't any "softies" in the family who will give in to your dog every time he whimpers, "More, please."

DIG THIS

Digging, which is seen as destructive behavior by most owners, is actually quite a natural behavior in dogs. When digging occurs in your yard, it is a normal behavior redirected into something the dog can do in his everyday life. In the wild, a dog would be actively seeking food, making his own shelter, etc. He would be using his paws in a purposeful manner for his survival. Because you provide him with food and shelter, he has no need to use his paws for these purposes, and so the energy that he would be using may manifest itself in the form of little holes all over your yard and flower beds.

Perhaps your dog is digging as a reaction to boredom—it's somewhat similar to someone eating a whole bag of chips in front of the TV simply because they are there and there is nothing better to do! Basically, the answer is to provide your dog with adequate play and exercise so that his mind and paws are occupied, and so that he feels as if he is doing something useful.

Of course, digging is easiest to control if it is stopped as soon as possible, but it is often hard to catch a dog in the act. If your dog is a compulsive digger and is not easily distracted by other activities, you can designate an area on your property where it is OK for him to dig. If you catch him digging in an off-limits area of the yard, immediately bring him to the approved area and praise him for digging there. Keep a close eye on him so that you can catch him in the act—that is the only way to make him understand what is permitted and what is not. If you take him to a hole he dug an hour ago and tell him "No," he will not understand that you are not fond of holes, or dirt, or flowers. If you catch him while he is stifle-deep in your tulips, that is when he will get your message.

If you don't want your Bulldog on the furniture, don't ever let him on it. Be consistent in your rules.

POOP ALERT!

Feces eating, aka coprophagia, is one of the most disgusting behavior that a dog could engage in, yet to the dog it is perfectly normal. Vets have found that diets with a low digestibility that contain relatively low levels of fiber and high levels of starch increase coprophagia. Therefore, high-fiber diets may decrease the likelihood of dogs' eating feces. To discourage this behavior, feed food that is nutritionally complete and in the proper amount. If changes in his diet do not work, and no medical cause can be found for stool-eating, you will have to modify the behavior through environmental control before it becomes a habit.

There are some tricks you can try, such as adding an unpleasant-tasting substance to the feces to make them unpalatable, or adding something to the dog's food that will make it unpleasant tasting after it passes through the dog. The best way to prevent your dog from eating his stool is to make it unavailable—clean up after he eliminates and remove any stool from the yard. If it is not there, he cannot eat it.

Never reprimand your dog for stool eating, as this rarely impresses the dog. Vets recommend distracting the dog while he is in the act of eating feces. Another option is to muzzle the dog when he is in the yard to relieve himself; this usually is effective within thirty to sixty days. Coprophagia most frequently is seen in pups six to twelve months of age, and usually disappears around the dog's first birthday.

AGGRESSION

This is the most obvious problem that concerns owners of Bulldogs. Aggression can be a very big problem in dogs, but more so in a dog with a fighting background. Aggression, when not controlled, always becomes dangerous. An aggressive dog, no matter the size, may lunge at, bite, or even attack a person or another dog.

Aggressive behavior is not to be tolerated. It is more than just inappropriate behavior; it is dangerous. It's painful for a family to watch their dog become unpredictable in his behavior to the point where they are afraid of him. While not all aggressive behavior is dangerous, growling, baring teeth, etc., can be frightening. It's important to ascertain why your dog is acting in this manner. Aggression is a display of dominance, and your dog should not have the dominant role in his pack, which in this case is your family.

It is important not to challenge an aggressive dog because this could provoke an attack. Observe your Bulldog's body language. Does he make direct eye contact and stare? Does he try to make himself as large as possible: ears pricked, chest out, neck arched? Height and size signify authority in a dog pack—being taller or "above" another dog literally means that he is "above" in the social status. These body signals tell you that your Bulldog thinks he is in charge, a problem that needs to be addressed.

An aggressive dog is unpredictable: you never know when he is going to strike, and what he is going to do. You cannot understand why a dog that is playful and loving one minute is growling and snapping the next minute.

Did You Know?

A relay race for dogs, flyball consists of a course of four hurdles leading to a levered box full of tennis balls. The team that correctly completes their run with the fastest time wins.

The best solution is to consult a behavioral specialist, preferably one who has experience with Bulldogs. Together, perhaps you can pinpoint the cause of your dog's aggression and do something about it. An aggressive dog cannot be trusted, and a dog that cannot be trusted is not safe to have as a family pet. If you find that your pet has become untrustworthy and you feel it necessary to seek a new home for him with a more suitable family and environment, explain fully to the new owners all your reasons for re-homing the dog.

AGGRESSION TOWARD DOGS

A dog's aggressive behavior toward another dog sometimes stems from insuffi-

SMART TIP!

Do not have long practice sessions with your Bulldog. He will become easily bored if you do. Also: Never practice when you are tired, ill, worried, or in a negative mood. This will transmit to your Bulldog and may have an adverse effect on his performance.

cient exposure to other dogs at an early age. In Bulldogs, early socialization with other dogs is essential. Bulldogs are not naturally aggressive toward other dogs; they have been bred down from a fighting dog to an loving house dog. It is the breeder and owner's responsibility to curb and redirect any signs of aggression so that the Bulldog

can become an upright member of canine society. If other dogs make your Bulldog nervous and agitated, he will lash out as a defensive mechanism, though this behavior is thankfully uncommon in the breed.

A dog who has not received sufficient exposure to other canines tends to believe that he is the only dog on the planet. The animal becomes so dominant that he does not even show signs that he is fearful or threatened. Without growling or any other physical signal as a warning, he will lunge at and bite another dog.

A way to correct this is to let your Bulldog approach another dog when walking on-leash. Watch closely and at the very first sign of aggression, correct your Bulldog and pull him away. Scold him for any sign of discomfort, and then praise him when he ignores or tolerates the other dog. Keep this up until he stops the aggressive behavior, learns to ignore the other dog, or accepts other dogs. Praise him lavishly for his correct behavior.

DOMINANT AGGRESSION

A social hierarchy is firmly established in a wild dog pack. The dog wants to dominate those under him and please those above him. Dogs know that there must be a leader.

it's a **Fact**

The calm, tolerant nature of the Bulldog makes him a perfect candidate for visiting people in hospitals, nursing homes, or mental-care facilities.

If you are not the obvious choice for emperor, your dog will assume the throne! These conflicting innate desires are what a dog owner is up against when he sets about training a dog. In training a dog to obey commands, the owner is reinforcing that he is the top dog in the pack and that the dog should, and should want to, serve his superior. Thus, the owner is suppressing the dog's urge to dominate by modifying his behavior and making him obedient.

An important part of training is taking every opportunity to reinforce that you are the leader. The simple action of making your Bulldog sit to wait for his food says that you control when he eats and that he is dependent on you for food. Although it may be difficult, do not give in to your dog's wishes every time he whines at you or looks at you with his pleading eyes. It is a constant effort to show your dog that his place in the pack is at the bottom.

This is not meant to sound cruel or inhumane. You love your Bulldog, and you should treat him with care and affection. You certainly did not get a dog just so you could boss around another creature. Dog training is not about being cruel or feeling important; it is about molding the dog's behavior into what is acceptable and teaching him to live by your rules. In theory, it is quite simple: catch him in appropriate behavior and reward him for it. Add a second dog into the equation and it becomes a bit more trying, but as a rule of thumb, positive reinforcement is what works best.

With a dominant dog, punishment and negative reinforcement can have the opposite effect of what you are after. It can make a dog fearful and/or act out aggressively if he feels he is being challenged. Remember, a dominant dog perceives himself to be at the top of the social heap and will fight to defend his perceived status. The best way to prevent that is never to give him reason to think that he is in control in the first place.

If you are having trouble training your Bulldog, and it seems as if he is constantly challenging your authority, seek the help of an obedience trainer or behavioral specialist. A professional will work with both you and your dog to teach you effective techniques to use at home. Beware of trainers who rely on excessively harsh methods; scolding is necessary now and then, but the focus in your training should always be on positive reinforcement.

If you can isolate what brings out the fear reaction, you can help your dog get over it.

Supervise your Bulldog's interactions with people and other dogs, and praise him when it goes well. If he starts to act aggressively in a situation, correct him and remove him from the situation. Do not let people approach your dog and start petting him without your express permission. That way, you can have your dog sit to accept petting, and praise him when he behaves properly. You are focusing on praise and on modifying his behavior by rewarding him when he acts appropriately. By being gentle and by supervising his interactions, you are showing him that there is no need to be afraid or defensive.

SEXUAL BEHAVIOR

To a certain extent, spaying/neutering will eliminate most sexual behaviors, but if you are purchasing a dog whom you wish to breed, you should be aware of what you will have to deal with throughout the dog's life.

Female dogs usually have two estruses (heat cycles) per year, with each season lasting about three weeks. These are the only times in which a female dog will mate, and she usually will not allow this until the second week of the cycle, but this varies from female to female. If not bred during the heat cycle, it is not uncommon for a female to experience a false pregnancy, in which her mammary glands swell, and she exhibits maternal tendencies toward toys or other objects.

Owners must further recognize that mounting is not merely a sexual expression but also one of dominance. Be consistent and persistent and you will find that you can "move mounters."

NOTABLE & QUOTABLE *The purpose of puppy classes is for the pups to learn how to learn. The pups get the training along the way, but the training is almost secondary.*—trainer Peggy Shunick Duezabou of Helena, Mont.

ABOUT BULLDOG

All dogs require some form of exercise, regardless of breed. A sedentary lifestyle is as harmful to a dog as it is to a person. Bulldogs are not an overly active breed, so you don't have to be very athletic to keep up with your Bulldog or keep him in shape!

Regular walks, play sessions in the yard, or letting your dog roam free in a safely enclosed area under your supervision are sufficient forms of exercise for your Bulldog. Bear in mind that an overweight dog should never be suddenly vigorously exercised; instead, he should be allowed to increase exercise slowly. Exercise is essential to keeping your dog's body fit and his mind sharp. A bored dog will find something to do, which often manifests itself in some type of destructive behavior. In this sense, exercise is essential for the owner's mental well-being, as well!

The great thing about Bulldogs is that they don't need a lot of room to roam, and they don't need to compete to feel complete. Spending the day with their owner is just fine with them, which is why, in addition to the normal dog sports of conformation, agility, and obedience, Bulldogs also rule on the social circuit in beauty pageants, on skateboards and even as mascots!

it's a Fact The Fédération Internationale Cynologique **is the world kennel club** that governs dog shows in Europe and elsewhere around the world.

Before You Begin
Because of the physical demands of sporting activities, a Bulldog puppy shouldn't begin officially training until he is done growing. That doesn't mean, though, that you can't begin socializing him to sports. Talk to your vet about what age is appropriate.

BULLDOGS AS BEAUTY PAGEANT CONTESTANTS?!

There's no real recipe for success for Bulldog beauty contests, though the funnier looking, friendlier, and more crazily dressed dogs do grab the judges' interest.

The Beautiful Bulldog Contest at Drake University in Des Moines, Iowa, whose mascot is the Bulldog, began on the last Monday in April 1978 and has been held each year since. The contest is held in conjunction with the Drake Relays, "America's Athletic Classic" event for track and field. Bulldog contestants come from several Midwestern states, including Minnesota, Nebraska, Illinois, Missouri, and Kansas. The contest has a cap of fifty Bulldog entries each year.

Another Bulldog beauty contest is held annually on Valentine's Day weekend in Long Beach, Calif., hosted by Justin Rudd, a pageant coach for the interview segments of Miss USA and Miss America contestants, and the host of www.hautedogs.org. The contest is often judged by real-life beauty queens and draws more than 300 contestants per year, and nearly 3,000 onlookers. Like the Drake contest, all the Bulldog needs to enter is a "pretty" face, lots of charm, great legs, and a friendly demeanor.

BOARDS FOR BULLIES

Just as some dogs are obsessed with playing fetch, some Bulldogs are obsessed with skateboarding. Whether skateboarding is a passion or just good fun for the

Bulldogs need to be active for the health of their body as well as their mind.

Bulldog, this breed seems to have a natural knack for this extreme sport.

No one is sure which Bulldog was the first to actually skateboard, but dozens of home videos featuring skateboarding Bulldogs can be found on the Internet. One of the funniest clips on the Internet dates back to 1988. In this skateboarding video excerpt, Lance Mountain, a professional skateboarder, is knocked off his skateboard, which is stolen by—what else? A Bulldog.

Of more recent fame—and perhaps the most famous skateboarding Bulldog—is a dog from Huntington Beach, Calif., named, Tyson. A fawn-and-white Bulldog, Tyson is known for his crazy speed and daring. He has made appearances on TV programs such as *American Idol, Rob & Big*, and *Oprah,* as well as TV commercials and programming aired in Japan, South Korea, and Australia.

Of course, female Bulldogs can skateboard, too, and perhaps the most recognized among the girls is Darla Belle, owned by Darrin Stout of South Pasadena, California. Darla, a white-with-brindle Bulldog, is a neighborhood favorite.

Chewing on the skateboard is not an uncommon behavior among skateboard-loving Bulldogs either and, according to the experts, the gnawing may be part of the pre-ride anticipation. And in case you might think chewing a board is a puppy thing, it's not. Tyson has the same habit. With Tyson, it's several minutes of "going crazy" over the board, flipping it over, chewing on the edges and barking before he settles into riding, says his owner, Jim Blauvelt.

THE BULLDOG AS MASCOT

If Bulldogs are so sweet-tempered, lovable, and not-so-athletic, why does this breed serve as a mascot for countless high school and college athletic teams, not to mention for the U.S. Marine Corps?

This stocky, blocky dog with muscular shoulders, stubby legs, and imposing jowls is probably one of the most recognizable breeds on the planet. Athletic teams from the University of Georgia to National University in the Philippines have adopted the Bulldog as their mascot—perhaps because they hope that the dog's intimidating appearance and reputed tenacity will inspire team members to perform in a similar fashion.

Although breeders have worked over many generations to eliminate aggressiveness from the Bulldog's temperament, the dog's legendary stubbornness is still an important part of his personality. That same refusal to give up, to let go, or to otherwise be diverted from the task at hand stands any football or athletic team—not to mention a military combat unit—in good stead.

Even one of the greatest human leaders of the 20th century, British Prime Minister Winston Churchill, found himself caricatured as a Bulldog on more than one occasion. The association is understandable. Like the Bully, Churchill had a squarish head, jowls, and a block-like stance. But it was Churchill's tenacity—his refusal to yield to Nazi Germany during World War II even after other

Despite what some people say, Bulldogs like water. Maybe not giant surf, but certainly fun and sun!

European nations had been forced to surrender—that earned him the gratitude of his countrymen and the rest of the world.

OBEDIENCE TRIALS

Obedience trials in the United States trace back to the early 1930s, when organized obedience training was developed to demonstrate how well dog and owner could work together. The pioneer of obedience trials is Mrs. Helen Whitehouse Walker, a Standard Poodle fancier, who designed a series of exercises after the Associated Sheep, Police Army Dog Society of Great Britain. Since the days of Mrs. Walker, obedience trials have grown by leaps and bounds, and today there are over 2,000 trials held in the United States every year, with more than 100,000 dogs competing. Any registered American Kennel Club or ILP (Indefinite Listing Privilege) dog can enter an obedience trial, regardless of conformational disqualifications or neutering.

Obedience trials are divided into three levels of progressive difficulty. At the first level, the Novice, dogs compete for the title Companion Dog; at the intermediate level, the Open, dogs compete for the title Companion Dog Excellent; and at the advanced level, dogs compete for the title Utility Dog. Classes are sub-divided into "A" (for beginners) and "B" (for more experienced handlers). A perfect score at any level is 200, and a dog must score 170 or better to earn a "leg," of which three are needed to earn the title. To earn points, the dog must score more than fifty percent of the available points in each exercise; the possible points range from twenty to forty.

Once a dog has earned the UD title, he can compete with other proven obedience dogs for the coveted title of Utility Dog Excellent, which requires that the dog win "legs" in ten shows. In 1977, the title Obedience Trial Champion was established by the AKC. Utility Dogs who earn "legs" in Open B and Utility B earn points toward their Obedience Trial Champion title. To become an OTCh., a dog needs to earn 100 points, which requires three first places in Open B and Utility under three different judges.

The Grand Prix of obedience trials, the AKC National Obedience Invitational, gives qualifying Utility Dogs the chance to win the newest and highest title: National Obedience Champion. Only the top twenty-five ranked obedience dogs, plus any dog ranked in the top three in his breed, are allowed to compete. •

AGILITY TRIALS

Agility is one of the most popular dog sports out there. Bulldogs are decent at this activity, though it requires speed (which Bulldogs are not known for!), precision, and obedience. If taken at his own pace, training your Bulldog in agility will boost his confidence and teach him to focus on you.

In agility competition, the dog and handler move through a prescribed course, negotiating a series of obstacles that may include jumps, tunnels, a dog walk, an A-frame, a seesaw, a pause table, and weave poles. Dogs that run through a course without refusing any obstacles, going off course, or knocking down any bars, all within a set time, get

SMART TIP!

Brachycephalic (short-nosed) breeds like Bulldogs already have issues with keeping cool on hot days. When you add an hour or two of intensive exercise in the heat, it can be really hard on these dogs. Take frequent "shade" breaks, and keep your Bulldog hydrated.

The Bulldog is more emotionally sensitive than many trainers expect, but he also has a high pain tolerance and stoic nature. Corrections generally have little effect, other than making him dislike training. Positive methods that encourage cooperation produce far better results.—Mary Jo Stabinski-Heckman, a trainer and breeder in Norristown, Pa.

a qualifying score. Dogs with a certain number of qualifying scores in their given division (Novice, Open, Excellent, and Mach at AKC trials) earn an agility title.

Several different organizations recognize agility events. AKC-sanctioned agility events are the most common. The United States Dog Agility Association also sanctions agility trials, as does the United Kennel Club. The rules are different for each of these organizations, but the principles are the same.

When Bulldogs compete in agility, they usually jump at a height that differs, depending on the height of the dog. With the exception of the jumps, Bulldogs are expected to negotiate the other obstacles on the course at the same height and distance as other breeds. Because each division of agility is subdivided by jump height, Bulldogs compete for ribbons against other dogs their own size.

When your Bulldog starts training for agility, he will begin by learning to negotiate each obstacle while on leash as you guide him. Eventually, you will steer him through a few obstacles in a row, one after another. Once he catches on that this is how agility works, he can run a short course off leash. One day, you'll see the light go on in his eyes as he figures out that he should look to you for guidance as he runs through a course. Your job will be to tell him which obstacles to take next, using your voice and your body as signals.

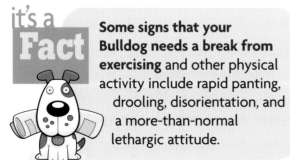

Some signs that your Bulldog needs a break from exercising and other physical activity include rapid panting, drooling, disorientation, and a more-than-normal lethargic attitude.

SHOW DOGS

When you purchase your Bulldog, you will make it clear to the breeder whether you want one just as a lovable companion and pet, or if you hope to buy a Bulldog with show prospects. No reputable breeder will sell you a young puppy and tell you that he is definitely of show quality because so much can go wrong during the early months of a puppy's development. If you plan to show your dog, what you will hopefully have acquired is a puppy with "show potential."

To the novice, exhibiting a Bulldog in the show ring may look easy, but it takes a lot of hard work and devotion to win blue ribbons at dog shows such as the prestigious Westminster Kennel Club dog show, not to mention a little luck, too!

The first concept that the canine novice learns when watching a dog show is that each dog first competes against members of his own breed. Once the judge has selected the best dog of each breed (Best of Breed) that dog will compete with other dogs in his group. Finally, the dogs chosen first in each group will compete for Best in Show.

The second concept that you must understand is that the dogs are not compared against one another. The judge compares each dog against his breed standard, the written description of the ideal specimen that is approved by the AKC. While some early breed standards were based on specific dogs who were famous or popular, many dedicated enthusiasts say that a perfect specimen, as described in the standard, has never walked into a show ring, has never been bred and, to the woe of dog breeders around the globe, does not exist. Breeders attempt to get as close to this ideal as possible with every litter, but theoretically the "perfect" dog is so elusive that it is impossible. (And if the "perfect" dog were

True Tails

As a Hollywood favorite, Bulldogs draw a wide and varied celebrity fan base, including comedian Adam Sandler, who is largely responsible for the current reign of Bulldog popularity in Hollywood.

Sandler's beloved Bulldog, Meatball, was best man at his wedding to model Jackie Titone in 2003. Footage of the dog wearing a tuxedo and a *yarmulke* while running down the aisle with the ring on a ring cushion strapped to his back is featured on Sandler's website (www.adam sandler.com), along with a wonderful tribute to this dog, who passed away from a heart attack in 2004. And there is a lot more doggie footage for fans to view of Meatball, as well as Sandler's next bulldog Matzoball, who passed away in 2008.

Matzoball was purported to go to work with Sandler, and judging by the number of photographs of the two-some around town and on the beach, they were inseparable, and the dog was very much a member of the Sandler household.

Sandler's love for the breed can be traced to his 2000 film *Little Nicky*, the story of Satan's son who comes to create hell on Earth, which Sandler co-wrote and co-produced. The movie features a Bulldog named Beefy, who was actually played by three different dogs trained by veteran Hollywood animal-actor trainer Steve Berens, who has been teaching animals the tricks of the movie trade for more than twenty years.

In 2008, Sandler found a new love in his third Bulldog, Babu.

SMART TIP!

Sports are physically demanding. Have your vet do a full examination of your Bulldog to rule out joint problems, heart disease, eye aliments, and other maladies. Once you get the all-clear healthwise, start having fun in your new sporting life!

born, breeders and judges probably would never agree that it was indeed "perfect.")

If you are interested in exploring the world of conformation, your best bet is to join your local breed club or the national (or parent) club, which is the Bulldog Club of America. These clubs often host both regional and national specialties, shows only for Bulldogs, which can include conformation as well as obedience and field trials. Even if you have no intention of competing with your Bulldog, a specialty is a like a festival for lovers of the breed who congregate to share their favorite topic: Bulldogs! Clubs also send out newsletters, and some organize training days and seminars in order for people may learn more about their chosen breed. To locate the Bulldog club closest to you, contact the AKC, which furnishes the rules and regulations for all of these events, plus general dog registration and other basic requirements of dog ownership.

On hot days, keep your Bulldog cool with wet towels when you're outside for long stretches of time. He overheats quickly!

The idea was to get a nice, quiet family dog, explains Ron Davis of Oxnard, Calif. The Davis family already owned a Rottweiler and a Rottie-mix, both adopted from the local shelter and both terrific family dogs. But for the next dog, they decided they'd like a smaller, calmer dog.

"We decided to go with a Bulldog because we wanted a well-mannered dog with a great temperament," Davis says. Tillman, a parti-colored Bulldog, was actually supposed to be a Mother's Day gift. "The deal was that she would pick the puppy, and I got to name him," Davis adds.

And how did the selection go? "Tillman is like a very short Lab; he's not a very calm dog at all," Davis laughs. In fact, Tillman is a bit obsessive—particularly when it comes to skateboarding. When out on his board, Tillman pumps with his paws to gather speed, leans and pushes his weight into corners, negotiates going down steps as expertly as a teenager, and when asked to come back to the truck to go home, "He puts his board down and skates off," Davis says with a sigh. "He's such a brat. I have to get on my board every time and go after him."

Even if you don't live in California, you might have seen Tillman. He's the Bulldog who was featured in an iPhone commercial, careening around streets on his skateboard. He has skateboarding videos posted on YouTube, and the dog even has his own website, www.gotillman.com. But his greatest claim to fame was as a contestant on the CBS reality show, *Greatest American Dog*. Fans of Tillman's antics can purchase stickers for their own skateboards and T-shirts, too.

Tillman learned by watching one of his "dog brothers." "Our Rottweiler, Stoli, had his own skateboard," Davis says. "He'd carry it around and push it all over the house. He'd get two paws up on it and push it up and down the street. When Tillman came into the house, the little guy would jump up on the board and stand on it. Stoli would let him have it." In order for the Rottweiler to have a skateboard, Davis had to go out and buy Tillman his own board. From there, Tillman pretty much figured things out on his own, riding his board next to Davis (on his own skateboard).

To find more information about this popular dog breed, contact the following organizations. They will be glad to help you dig deeper into the world of the Bulldog.

American College of Veterinary Nutrition: www.acvn.org

American Kennel Club: The AKC website offers information and links to conformation, rally, obedience and agility programs, and member clubs: www.akc.org

Bulldog Club of America: This club is the parent club of the AKC. The site includes breed information, breeder referral, and more: www.thebca.org

Canadian Kennel Club: Our northern neighbor's oldest kennel club is similar to the AKC in the states: www.ckc.ca

Canine Performance Events: Get your Bulldog started in agility: www.k9cpe.com

North American Dog Agility Council: This site provides links to clubs, trainers, and agility trainers in the United States and Canada: www.nadac.com

The Bulldog Club of America Rescue Network: This nonprofit organization has volunteers nationwide who love the Bulldog breed and are dedicated to its continued well-being. www.rescuebulldogs.org

it's a
Fact
The **American Kennel Club** was started in 1884. It is America's oldest kennel club. The **United Kennel Club** is the second oldest in the United States. It began registering dogs in 1898.

Tillman, the Skateboarding Bulldog: This site contains videos of one of the most famous skateboarding bulldogs around: Tillman, from the reality show, *Greatest American Dog*: www.gotillman.com

Tyson, the Skateboarding Bulldog: This site contains videos of another skateboarding Bulldog: Tyson: www.skateboardingbulldog.com

United Kennel Club: This kennel club, the second oldest in the United States, offers several of the same events offered by the AKC, including agility, conformation, and obedience. In addition, the UKC offers competitions in hunting and dog sport (companion and protective events). Both the UKC and the AKC offer programs for juniors, ages 2 to 18: www.ukcdogs.com

United States Dog Agility Association: The USDAA has information on training, clubs, and events in North America and overseas: www.usdaa.com

BOARDING

So you want to take a family vacation—and you want to include all members of the family. You would probably make arrangements for accommodations ahead of time anyway, but this is especially important when traveling with a dog. You do not want to make an overnight stop at the only place around for miles and find out that the hotel does not allow dogs. Also, you don't want to reserve a room for your family without confirming that you are traveling with a dog because if it's against the hotel's policy, you may not have a place to stay.

Alternatively, if you are traveling and choose not to bring your Bulldog, you will have to make arrangements for him. Some options are to bring him to a family member's or neighbor's house, to have a trusted neighbor stop by often or stay at your house, or to bring your dog to a reputable boarding kennel.

If you choose to board him at a kennel, you should visit in advance to see the facilities and see how clean they are and where the dogs are kept. Talk to the employees and see how they treat the dogs—do they spend time with the dogs, play with them, exercise them? Also

find out the kennel's policy on vaccinations and what is required. This is for the dogs' safety because when dogs are kept together, there is a greater risk of diseases being passed from dog to dog.

Traveling with your Bulldog can be a blast if you plan ahead.

HOME STAFFING

For the Bulldog parent who works all day, a pet sitter or dog walker may be the perfect solution for the lonely dog longing for a mid-day stroll. Owners can approach local high schools or community centers if they don't know of a neighbor interested in a part-time commitment. Interview potential dog walkers and consider their experience with dogs, as well as your Bulldog's rapport with the candidate. (Bulldogs are excellent judges of character, unless there's liver involved.) Always check references before entrusting your dog and home to a dog walker.

For an owner's long-term absence, such as a three-day business trip or a one-week vacation to the islands, many Bulldog owners welcome the services of a pet sitter. It's usually less stressful on the dog to stay home with a pet sitter than to be boarded in a kennel. Pet sitters also may be more affordable than a week's stay at a full-service doggie day care.

Pet sitters must be even more reliable than dog walkers, as the dog is depending on his surrogate owner for all of his needs for an extended period. Smart owners are advised to hire a certified pet sitter through the National Association of Professional Pet Sitters, which can be accessed online at www.petsitters.org. NAPPS provides online and toll-free pet sitter locator services. The nonprofit organization only certifies serious-minded, professional individuals who are knowledgeable in behavior, nutrition, health, and safety. Always keep your Bulldog's best interest at heart when planning a trip.

If you're going away for more than a day, consider hiring a pet sitter to care for your dog.

SCHOOL'S IN SESSION

Puppy kindergarten, which is usually open to puppies between three to six months of age, allows puppies to learn and socialize with other dogs and people in a structured setting. Classes help your Bulldog enjoy going places with you, and help your dog become a well-behaved member at public gatherings that include other dogs. They prepare him for adult obedience classes, as well as for life.

The problem with most puppy kindergarten classes is that they only occur one night a week. What about during the rest of the week?

If you're at home all week, you may be able to find other places to take your puppy, but you have to be careful about dog parks and other places where just any dog can go. An experience with a bully can undo all the good your classes have done, or worse, end in tragedy.

If you work, your puppy may be home alone all day. Chances are he can't hold himself that long, so your potty training will be undermined unless you're just aiming to teach him to use an indoor potty. And chances are, by the time you come home, he'll be so bursting with energy that you may start feeling that he's hyperactive.

SMART TIP!

Remember to keep your dog's leash slack when interacting with other dogs. It is not unusual for a dog to pick out one or two canine neighbors to dislike. If you know there's bad blood, step off to the side and put a barrier, such as a parked car, between the dogs. If there are no barriers to be had, move to the side of the walkway, cue your dog to sit, stay, and watch you until his nemesis passes; then continue your walk.

The answer? Doggie day care. Most larger cities have some sort of day care, whether it's a boarding kennel that keeps your dog in a run or a full-service day care that offers training, play time, and even spa facilities. Doggie day cares range in style from a person who keeps a few dogs at his or her home to a state-of-the-art facility built just for dogs. Many of the more sophisticated doggie day cares offer webcams so that you can watch out for your dog throughout the day.

Look for:
- escape-proof facilities, including a buffer between the dogs and any doors
- inoculation requirements for new dogs
- midday meals for young dogs
- obedience training (if offered), using reward-based methods
- safe and comfortable time-out areas for sleeping
- screening of dogs for aggression
- small groups of similar sizes and ages
- toys and playground equipment such as tunnels
- trained staff, with an adequate number to supervise the dogs (no more than ten to fifteen dogs per person)
- a webcam

CAR TRAVEL

You should accustom your Bulldog to riding in a car at an early age. You may or may not take him in the car often, but at the very least he will need to go to the vet, and you do not want these trips to be traumatic for your dog or troublesome for you. The safest way for a Bulldog to ride in the car is in his crate. If he uses a crate in the house, you can use the same crate for travel.

Another option is a specially made safety harness for dogs, which straps the dog in much like a seat belt. Do not let your dog roam loose in the vehicle—this is very dangerous! If you should stop short, your Bulldog can be thrown and injured. If your dog starts climbing on you and pestering you while you are driving, you will not be able to concentrate on the road. It is an unsafe situation for everyone—human and canine.

For long trips, be prepared to stop to let your dog relieve himself. Take with you whatever you need to clean up after him, including some paper towels and perhaps some old bath towels should he have an accident in the car or suffer from motion sickness.

Did You Know?

The dog run is one of the few urban spaces where a dog can be off-leash. To enter, dogs must be fully vaccinated and healthy, and females must not be in season.

IDENTIFICATION

Your Bulldog is your valued companion and friend. That is why you must always keep a close eye on him, and this also is why you have made sure that he cannot escape from the yard or wriggle out of his collar and run away from you.

However, accidents can happen, and there may come a time when your dog unexpectedly gets separated from you. If this unfortunate event should occur, proper identification, including an ID tag, a tattoo, and possibly a microchip, will increase the chances of his being returned to you safely and quickly.

An ID tag on a collar or harness is the primary means of pet identification (and ID licenses are required in many communities, anyway). Although inexpensive and easy to read, collars and ID tags can come off or be taken off.

A microchip doesn't get lost. Containing a unique ID number that can be read by a scanner, the microchip is embedded under the pet's skin. It's invaluable for identifying lost or stolen pets. However, to be effective, the chip must be registered in a national database, and owner contact info kept up-to-date. Additionally, not every shelter or veterinary clinic has a scanner, nor do most folks who might pick up and try to return the lost pet. Best bet: Get both!

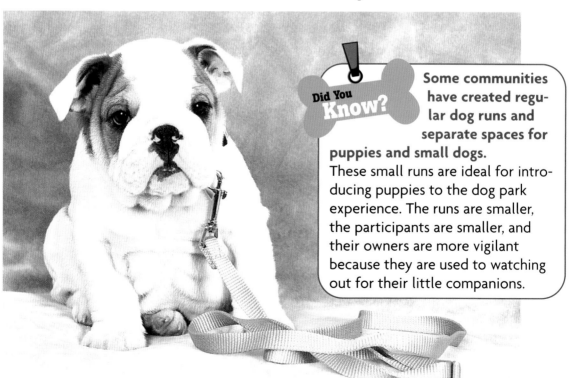

Did You Know? Some communities have created regular dog runs and separate spaces for puppies and small dogs. These small runs are ideal for introducing puppies to the dog park experience. The runs are smaller, the participants are smaller, and their owners are more vigilant because they are used to watching out for their little companions.

INDEX